'I never knew either of my grandfathers, and neither, to all intents and purposes, did my own children, so when Archie was born and I became a grandparent myself, I was determined to enjoy the relationship with him.

It wasn't difficult. I had been in a state of acute excitement as soon as I heard he, or she, existed. Well before he or she was born I knew that his or her presence was going to change my life quite significantly.

Archie is now nearly two and there has not been a moment when my love or affection for him has wavered. I relish the time I have with him. I am quite happy to slow my own life down to the pace of his. These are not obsessive or possessive feelings, and I'm quite aware they may not last, but, for now, it's nice to be around someone who brings out all the good things one is capable of.'

Michael Palin, March 2008

The Modern GRANDPARENTS' GUIDE

JACKIE HIGHE

PIATKUS

PIATKUS

First published in Great Britain in 2008 by Piatkus Books

A CIP catalogue record for this book
is available from the British Library

ISBN 978-0-7499-0951-2

Illustrated by Chris Duggan
Text design by Goldust Design
Typeset in Bembo by Goldust Design
Printed and bound in Great Britain by CPI Mackays, Chatham, ME5 8TD

Papers used by Piatkus Books are natural, renewable and recyclable
products made from wood grown in sustainable forests and certified
in accordance with the rules of the Forest Stewardship Council.

Piatkus Books
An imprint of
Little, Brown Book Group
100 Victoria Embankment
London EC4Y 0DY

An Hachette Livre UK Company
www.hachettelivre.co.uk

www.piatkus.co.uk

Jackie Highe is an experienced hands-on grandmother, and one of the top women's magazine editors in Britain. For fourteen years she was Editor-in-Chief of *Bella*, then Britain's biggest selling weekly magazine. Her previous book, *Now, Where Did I Put My Glasses?*, about caring for your elderly parents, was published in 2007.

This book is dedicated, with love, to my five wonderful granddaughters: Madeleine Rose, Alice Sophie, Daisy Yi-Xin, Verity Yi-Én and Susanna Lucy.

Contents

Acknowledgements

I would like to express my gratitude to all those grandparents, parents and grandchildren, both friends and strangers (until now), who spoke to me so frankly and let me into their lives. Their honesty and generosity have enabled me to fill the book with wonderful stories. The humour, dedication and downright courage they reveal, is testimony to the marvel that is a twenty-first-century grandparent.

My thanks go to Pat Argue and other friends, who helped to make some of those stories possible by connecting me with *their* friends, and to Alan Brooke and Denise Dwyer, my editors at Piatkus, for their complete support and empathy. Thank you too, to my literary agent and friend, Doreen Montgomery of Rupert Crew Ltd, for being behind me all the way – and for her hawk-like subbing eye!

I'd also like to say a word of thanks for all the vital organisations which exist to help and support grandparents in the many complex, sometimes harrowing, situations they can face – charities like Grandparents Apart and Grandparents Plus and in particular the Grandparents Association, for their knowledge and helpfulness.

Introduction

As I write these words, I'm anticipating the arrival of our five granddaughters, aged from nine to three, for a weekend without their parents. Little girls they may be, but they'll descend on the house like a tidal wave, and everything will go down before them. For two days no jobs will be done, no rest will be taken. Perhaps at some point I'll manage to give the kitchen floor a hasty sweep, and their granddad might possibly get the grass cut, but it's a toss-up and, in any case, they'll be deeply involved in both chores.

We'll probably take them for a long, long walk up the nearest hill, and eat apples and chocolate at the top. Or we might go to the zoo and take a picnic. On Saturday at teatime we're bound to have a family disco in the living room. And I expect I'll have to give them what they call a 'spa day' (really a spa hour), when five small sets of fingers and toes make their appearance on the kitchen table for me to glamourise with varnish. But first, they'll spend at least twenty minutes making their colour selections from my supplies. I'll have to paint samples onto paper . . .

In the intervals between all these activities, the girls will cover the back path, patio and garden with the bits and pieces of an elaborate, weekend-long piece of make-believe, and litter the interior of the house with the props for various other games. At some point they'll no doubt put on a 'show' for us, and in the run-up to that they'll disembowel the dressing-up box and parade round in an exotic collection of cast-offs, striking attitudes and poses, inventing stories about their costumes and concocting elaborate plots.

While they're here, all semblance of 'normal' life will cease. We'll loosen our stays and just enjoy whatever happens. On Sunday afternoon, when they've devoured whatever their favourite meal of the moment turns out to be, and gone home, we'll leave the debris and have a lie-down. Then we'll start the process of reclaiming the house, smiling at the things they've said and done, storing up the memories. That's modern grandparenting. It's fabulous.

How different it is from the time we spent with our own grandparents. Back then, far from making cool moves with them to a CD of the Darkness, we'd have been expected to sit quietly. We couldn't have made a mess, because there were no toys at their houses to make a mess with. We may have been allowed to dress up, but I can't imagine any of *my* grand-parents watching a show, and smiling while I paraded naked (apart from a headdress) in my role as a slave girl. My grand-mothers were lovely, and I loved them, but they wouldn't have approved of nudity. And I can't see them painting my nails – it's an impossible vision.

They seemed ancient. Whatever their actual age, they looked, behaved, and no doubt *felt*, ancient. They threw on age as a mantle, embraced it, became staid, dignified and developed a gravitas that would never have allowed them to party with their grandchildren in the way that we do now. It wouldn't have crossed their minds – even if they'd been fit enough. They'd taken a back seat in life.

Twenty-first-century grandparents are the opposite. The

baby-boom generation is young – physically, mentally and actually. There are currently 13 million grandparents in the UK, and one in two people have grandchildren by the time they're fifty-four.

Becoming a grandparent for the first time is a leap into the unknown. You wake up one morning to find you've moved up the generation chain. Suddenly you have to see yourself in a new light and, however keen you are to have grandchildren, it's a shock to the system. Others might not regard you in a different way, but your image of yourself will change. You won't be putting in a bulk order for thermal underwear, or exchanging your stilettos for sensible shoes – you won't be turning into *your* grandparents – but you'll have a new position in the family. There's another small life that will depend on you for – what? – just about anything. In fact, practically everything at some time or another. It's exciting, but perhaps a little scary, too. You need to get your head round it

Whether you've been anticipating this for years, or hoping it wouldn't happen quite yet, the moment you meet your first grandchild is unlike anything you've experienced so far in your life: truly magical. However many grandchildren you have, each one will weave the same spell. It's as though a light flicks on somewhere and you're flooded with a new emotion – devotion. They bring it with them, and now you've got it for life. You might have the imagination of a Charles Dickens, but you can have no conception of how this feels until it happens to you. It's incredible. The rush of love is spontaneous and unstoppable, and it gives your life a new purpose and meaning.

These days, we're all healthier, bounding with energy, and living longer. That's wonderful – and it's just as well, because grandparents have an important role to play. The last fifty years have seen colossal changes in attitudes and expectations, and this has made a profound difference to family life. Grandparents today face challenges that didn't tax our predecessors.

We fill the emotional gaps left by stressed-out parents who are working long hours to pay their way; and we take on the childcare to save them cash. There are more divorces than ever before, more single parents, more extended families, and it's increasingly falling to grandparents to hold these fragments together, to provide an anchor for grandchildren who may be estranged from one or both of their parents – and to help our children through it, too.

We may have the energy for all this, but perhaps not enough hours in a day: many of us are working full-time; we're still caught up in our own lives. Because we're young, retirement might be a long way in the future and, anyway, the statutory retirement age is rising. We're called upon for so many things and in so many ways that we can find ourselves under enormous pressure.

What do you do, for example, if your child's marriage breaks down and you find their partner punishes *you*, and won't allow you to see your grandchildren any longer? What does the law say? Is there any way you can prevent this disaster from happening in the first place? What should you do if you suspect your grandchild is taking drugs? What if your children and grandchildren live on the other side of the world?

It's not just these huge things – there are plenty of less dramatic issues which have always stressed grandparents and their children: when (not) to interfere; when to speak up and when to stay silent; how to agree on discipline/spoiling. They sound commonplace, but they can blow up into unpleasant little upsets surprisingly easily. They're delicate issues, all pieces of the patchwork that makes up a grandparent's life.

It's an adventure and, like any adventure, as well as thrills and excitement, it has its share of traps for the unwary, its dangers and risks. Whether you're lucky enough to be part of a close, loving family, or yours has split wide open, this book is your guide through all the aspects of being a grandparent in the third millennium; its ramifications and complexities, marvels and miracles. It will keep you up to speed on the many changes in thinking that have taken place since you were a parent; give you the poise and the knowledge to succeed in this balancing act; it will help with fundamental issues – feeding the faddy, calming a new mother's storms – all the little everyday things you'll find yourself handling; it will walk you through the legalities of custody and rights of access. It will take you on a journey that begins when your first grandchildren are born, right through to when they're teenagers.

I've spoken to dozens of grandparents, parents – and grandchildren, too. Their stories provide a unique perspective – first-hand experience of everything from having grandchildren to stay for a weekend, to becoming a full-time parent to your own grandchild. They're warm and funny, revealing, poignant – sometimes shocking and tragic. They bring to life the heart-searching and insecurities, the courage, determination, simple love and absolute joy which encompass being a grandparent today.

At the end of each chapter (and in the resources at the back of the book) are practical guides to give you the information and resources you need to get on top of the game and stay there: contacts, support groups, help lines, guides to the law.

I can't imagine a greater privilege than being a grandparent. Our hearts are elastic – each time a new grandchild is born, they expand to hold it. One of my granddaughters asked me recently which of them is my favourite. I said I didn't have a favourite – that I love them *all* the most, and that even if I had another twenty grandchildren, I'd still love them all the most.

Whatever the circumstances of individual families, whatever ups and downs we have to face, grandparents cope because that love sees us through. Of course we want to be perfect – we want to be the best grandparents there have ever been, just as we wanted to be the best parents. But here's the truth – we don't need to try too hard. The stories in this book prove that we're naturally talented, we come with the software installed. In our way, all of us are already perfect.

1

A New Experience

Once upon a time, grandparents were old. They didn't just seem that way to their grandchildren because of the age difference between them – they *acted* old. Only two generations ago couples who had barely reached their middle sixties sat at opposite sides of the fireplace in fluffy slippers listening to *Mrs Dale's Diary*. Grandmothers polished their brass plaques to the strains of *Music While You Work* on the Light Programme, and crocheted antimacassars for the backs of sofas. Grandfathers played golf or dug the allotment, pottered about in the shed and never missed the gardening tips on the Home Service.

We might have loved our grandparents, but often we didn't know them very well because when they were around we had to be on our best behaviour. There was a lingering Victorian feel to their attitudes and lifestyle, a whiff of horsehair sofas. And they might have loved *us* but, however gentle and kind they were, mostly they didn't roll around on the floor with us or take us swimming on Saturday afternoons.

In fact we probably never saw them undressed, even on the beach. After having lots of children most women's figures were effectively wrecked, so they covered up in shapeless dresses, wore opaque stockings all year round and lace-up shoes with stacked heels as *their* mothers had done. Many grandfathers, like *their* fathers, routinely wore trilbies and three-piece suits on weekdays, even when they were retired. At weekends they tended to favour cardigans and grey flannel trousers – but still with a collar and tie.

Of course these are generalisations, but for many of us facing the possibility or the reality of grandparenthood now, it's a glimpse of the way the world was, and had been for generations. You grew up, got married and had children. When they had children, that was it – you grew old.

But *we're* not old. Today fifty is the new forty; sixty is the new forty-five. We play CDs by Queen and the Clash; we saw the Beatles at the Cavern; we download Coldplay and Scissor Sisters onto our iPods. We're cool. Grandmothers might still wear opaque tights and high-heeled lace-ups, but only when the fashion magazines say it's chic; grandfathers have abandoned flannel bags for chinos, and they man the barbecue in cut-offs, flip-flops and baseball caps. Grandparents might still play golf and stake the dahlias, but that's in-between holding down a job, cycling round France, hiking in Bhutan and shopping online for computer add-ons.

So how do we equate this with having grandchildren?

Unlike our predecessors, we're not ready to hand on the burden of active life – we're still living it. We don't feel our time is up, or over, or out. We might be delighted to welcome a new generation into our lives, but those lives remain just that – ours. Whether we're ready to embrace it with open arms, or slightly dreading it as a visible sign that we're over the hill, one thing is certain – we won't be approaching the role in the way our grandparents did. Life still holds too many temptations, possibilities and adventures for us to sink quietly into rocking chairs.

That can only be a good thing. We can share those adventures with our grandchildren. We're young enough in body and spirit to do all those things our predecessors didn't do and more – much more. We can take them swimming – heck, we can take them scuba diving, surfing, sailing, snorkelling. We can go off with them on bicycles or horseback, or strap them into our people carriers and disappear to Spain for the school holidays. We can queue our way round Disneyland, scream our way down a rollercoaster, squelch our way through petting zoos. We can teach them to hand jive, tell them about *our* teenage trips to rock festivals. And all the time we're drawing closer together, sharing, experiencing.

The relationships we forge with our grandchildren will have an added dimension because we've got the best of both worlds: a fascinating foot in the past and a vibrant presence in the here and now. It's fantastic.

Are We Ready For This?

However much we might love our children, the concept of being a grandparent can take some getting used to. That's because it's the end of an era. From being young parents at the centre of our children's lives, going through the process of helping them grow up, leave home and strike out on their own, suddenly we have to face the fact that they're forming not just a separate life, but a new tribe – one we don't lead.

Some people might feel it's a kind of displacement, as though they're being moved slightly out of the picture, and worry that as a result they might not be taken so seriously as a person.

Cameron, who's a widower, admits he had mixed feelings when his daughter Grace told him she was pregnant. 'I was fifty-two and working with a lot of younger men. I'd never had a problem with our relative ages or felt any different from the other blokes, but as soon as they heard about the baby they started to call me granddad. I hated it. I could still do everything they could do – and better! Grace told me not to be so daft. She said, "Just wait till the baby arrives – you'll forget all this macho stuff." And I did. Pearl is six now and she can get me to do anything – anything at all. I'm a complete idiot with her. I don't care who calls me granddad now because *she* does – that's what I am and proud of it.'

Cameron was worried that underneath the leg-pulling he was already being considered a back number. His job needs him to be tough, fit and resourceful, and to command the respect and cooperation of his colleagues, and he was afraid that his age, which hadn't been an issue, was suddenly being highlighted. It's understandable – in fact he'd probably been worrying anyway without admitting it to himself, and his daughter's pregnancy brought him face to face with it. But once his granddaughter was born, he realised it hadn't made any difference at all – he was still the same person.

Freddie is worried about his image too – at forty-four he feels he's too young to be a grandfather. His second wife, Cleo, is thirteen years his elder and her children are a decade older than his. Her son's first child, Molly, is seven months old. He says:

It's come to me earlier than I anticipated. My own son is just seventeen. Do I qualify as a granddad? I don't like the idea of that. I'm moving into this place where I'm in the winter of my years – I know that's an old-fashioned image, but it's how I feel. I suppose it's frighteningly vain but 'Granddad' isn't how I want to be seen socially.

Of course I'm pleased for Cleo, but I didn't sign up to be a step-grandparent – not yet anyway. When we got together we thought about all the other aspects of our age difference, but funnily enough we never considered this. I shall be a completely supportive and polite partner to Cleo but I've yet to hold Molly. I don't really do babies anyway. I can't see me describing myself as a granddad.

Freddie doesn't feel he's reached the stage in his own life where being a grandparent should be a prospect, and now he's having to come to terms with the role. It's fair enough – lots of men his age are only just starting their own families. But once he realises that this 'old codger' image is out of date, that *he* hasn't changed, he might see what he's missing by taking a back seat and start to be more hands on. And having such a young grandfather is going to be wonderful for Molly as she grows up.

It's not just grandfathers who can fight shy of the idea. Monica is fifty-seven and her daughter Rose is pregnant with her first child. 'I'm not sure how I feel. I don't think I was a great mum – I worked full-time and didn't give up everything for my children. In some ways I'm quite selfish. I've always managed to find time for myself, and I still have a full-time job. I'm not desperate to have this happen. I'll just have to wait and see.' Monica shouldn't feel guilty about finding time for herself – everyone needs that. It won't necessarily have made her a bad parent; on the contrary, it might have helped to make her a good, balanced one, and it will have the same effect when she's a grandmother. And you don't need to be desperate for a grandchild in order to love it when it arrives.

Linda is sixty-six and semi-retired. She has what she describes as a 'lovely life'.

> I enjoy my job, my friends and my freedom. Since my husband died, I've become colossally selfish. I can do what I like when I like. I sit in my garden reading and I can hear next door's grandchildren playing and my neighbours rushing about after them, and I think – thank goodness that's not me. Oh, I'd like grandchildren, but I have to admit that I wouldn't want to have them every day; once a week would be quite enough. They're a mixed blessing. I'm used to having my home tidy – it's the way I like it and I think I'd be the kind of granny who hid away my things before they came to visit me.

Linda isn't sure about how much she'd like grandchildren to disrupt her orderly life, and so she's wondering whether that means she really wants them, and how good she'd be with them. But the fact that she's thought about it at all proves she'll be able to sort it out when the time comes. There is no standard of perfection for a grandparent – only the way you want and need to be.

Sometimes hesitation is due to other concerns. Jane and Sam were worried when their daughter Kirsty became pregnant. Sam says:

> Kirsty was only eighteen – it was a traumatic time. We were shocked and just a little bit disappointed because we'd had

such hopes for her, and we were concerned about what this baby would do to her life. But she gave up work and married her boyfriend, Eric. We knew and liked him, and they'd intended to get married eventually – just not quite so soon! Of course we gave her as much practical help as possible, although we couldn't afford a lot financially. She knew we were here whenever she wanted us. Eric's mother was very good about it too – she'd married under the same circumstances so she completely understood. Kirsty and Eric are doing fine – they have two little boys now and we're delighted. We feel very privileged.

It was natural for Jane and Sam to worry about their daughter's future, but they faced facts and did what they could to help make her life easier. But what if you don't much like your child's partner and they say they're having a child together? Babs and George's son Luke had been living with his partner, Belinda, for four years when they announced they were having a baby. George says:

We were completely dismayed. We've tried, but we've never much liked Belinda. We think she's selfish and spoilt and doesn't really care about Luke, and we knew they'd been having problems. To be really frank we were hoping they'd split up. We kept thinking that one day he'd see her as she really is and walk away.

When they told us about the baby I'm sure they expected us to make a big fuss – you know, scream and throw our arms round them, but it was all we could do to look pleased, never mind enthusiastic. If you could have read the bubble over our heads it would have said, 'Oh no, they'll always be linked now.' What an awful thing to be thinking! I could see they were a bit taken down, so I made a huge effort and hugged Belinda, and the moment passed. Now Sian's born we love her to bits of course, but it hasn't changed the fact that we think Belinda's not right for Luke. We feel it's wrong to have a baby to mend a dodgy relationship, but how could we tell them that? Now we can't *hope* for them to split up, can we? And they're talking about marrying next year.

George and Babs can't really know what their son's relationship with Belinda is like – and even if they're right about her faults, it isn't their business. What matters is what Luke thinks of her and how they feel about each other. It's true that a baby doesn't work like magic glue to mend the cracks in a relationship, but apart from being there for their son, George and Babs's job now, as grandparents, is to make sure that whatever happens in the future they're a loving, stable presence for Sian.

We can't control what our children do – or at what stage they do it, and this is something Harriet has found out the hard way. She's desperate to have grandchildren, but her daughter Chrissie isn't ready to start a family yet – if at all.

Chrissie doesn't want to interrupt her life for babies. At thirty-five she's at the top of her career and enjoying it. I think if she leaves it too late she'll regret it and be terribly sorry later and, in fact, I've said that to her, but I don't harp on – we have a good relationship and I don't want to do anything that would jeopardise it. But women who have babies very late run a far greater risk – to their own health and to that of the baby – and I worry about that too. That's another reason I don't go on about it any more; what if I did manage to persuade Chrissie and then she had a handicapped baby – she might blame me.

When I *have* brought babies up she just says, 'But, Mum,

I'm not married, and I'm not in the kind of relationship where a baby would be a good idea – you need to be completely committed for that.' She's right. But then again, I admit to myself it's not just her I'm thinking about – I know I want it for me, too. I wouldn't want her to have a baby whose presence she resented, of course not, but I feel hugely impoverished. I can't ask to cuddle the children of friends – and these days you can't even speak to children unless you know them. Having grandchildren immeasurably enriches your life. I'd be a doting grandma, but rational – I wouldn't give them toys, I'd give them time. I think about what we'd do together, how we'd be. I'd love them so much. I've got lots to give.

If Harriet looks at her daughter's life dispassionately, leaving her own needs out of the picture, she'll see that Chrissie is thinking things through. From her point of view what she's doing makes perfect sense. You don't have children for your parents' sake (would *you* have done?), you have them when you're ready, when the time seems right for you. And if you choose not to have them at all, well, it's your life.

Deep down Harriet realises that and she's stopped pushing before she causes a rift.

How much you can say to your daughter – or daughter-in-law for that matter – depends on the closeness of the relationship you have with her. But Harriet needs to remind herself that this is not her decision to make. She's done all she can as a mother – maybe too much – by pointing out her concerns. Certainly anything more would be inappropriate. Harriet loves her daughter and she has to allow Chrissie to decide what's best for her life and to face up to what that might mean for her own.

Chrissie isn't unusual in wanting to wait before having children. It's common now for first babies to be born to women in their thirties and early forties, because many couples are making lasting relationships later in life. In the 1960s and 1970s it was normal to marry and have babies at a young age – girls were routinely leaving school at sixteen, marrying at eighteen and having their 2.4 children before their twenty-third birthday. Teenagers who went on to further education still tended to have their children in their early and middle twenties. These days, couples frequently don't marry at all and, if they do, it's often as a prelude to starting a family. That means wishful grandparents have to wait – sometimes longer than they want to.

When Hannah and Derek got married, Derek's mother, Lana, was confidently expecting a baby to follow quickly.

We'd been together for six years, and Mum had dropped a few hints about having kids, but we'd brushed them aside fairly casually. It wasn't something we wanted to think about. But almost as soon as the wedding was over she started on at Hannah: 'When are you going to give me a grandchild, then?'

Hannah was quite sympathetic at first – I'm an only child and Dad's been dead for years, so I'm all Mum's got. But she kept going on about it. It got so that every time we saw her she'd bring it up. She didn't get heavy, just all these little hints and half jokes – 'When I'm a grandma I won't be able to dash off at a moment's notice, so I'm going on holiday next week,' that kind of thing. It drove Hannah mad – after all, her own mum wasn't like that.

Eventually Hannah blew up. She told Mum to mind her own business, that we'd have a child if and when we wanted one, not a baby to order. It shut Mum up. She was really upset. I've never seen her so hurt, but I had to back Hannah – she was right. She said to me – what kind of a grandma is she going to be if she's like this *now*?

We didn't start trying for a baby until our third wedding anniversary – we weren't really able to afford to consider it until then. It took another two years before we had our son Ryan, and Mum was overjoyed. I think she'd given up hoping. She's turned out to be a pretty good gran as it happens.

Hannah lashed out at her mother-in-law because she wouldn't let the subject drop. What had been light-hearted banter with a little bit of intent became intrusive when it was always being mentioned. If she couldn't stop herself from bringing it up in the first place, then it would have been better to mention it once and leave it there.

If you're tempted to start dropping hints about babies, imagine how you'd have felt if your parents or in-laws had done it to you (maybe they did). Outraged? Invaded? Undermined? It's your children's decision, just as it was yours, and they have the right to make it. Be cool. The fact is, you can't change things to suit yourself – really, you can't. And if you think about it, why would you want to? After all, you love your children and you want them to be happy – their way.

Helen didn't believe it when her daughter Phoebe told her she was pregnant, because they didn't expect grandchildren at all.

Robert and I always believed Phoebe would be a career woman. She was married, but at twenty-six, after four years at Oxford, she still hadn't done a lot with her life. I thought she'd want to live a bit and get some experience in her career so, although I love babies, I didn't imagine they would be on the agenda. When her husband's job took them to the Far East we thought that was that.

Then one day she phoned me from Malaysia and said,

'Mum, I'm going into the baby business.' Pregnancy was so far from my mind I thought she meant she was opening a shop or something, and my feeling was – what a waste after all those years at Oxford. So I said, not very joyfully, 'Oh.' There was a moment's silence and then the penny dropped and Phoebe said, 'No, I mean I'm having one!' Apparently they'd been planning it this way, because they were going to come home in time for the baby to be born. Our daughter's very organised – we're kept pretty much in the dark. We get to hear about plans after they're made.

Helen has the right attitude – let them get on with it. It can pay dividends, too. Hazel's daughter Nadine had been married for fifteen years with no sign of a baby. 'Nadine and Tom got married when they were only nineteen and twenty, so I didn't expect them to rush into having children. Time went on and I was keen, but I never once said anything. I was quietly worried they might be having trouble conceiving, but I thought it was their business. For all I knew they were trying like mad. It wouldn't have helped to have me pushing, would it? Then Nadine appeared on the doorstep one day and just said, "I'm pregnant." We both burst into tears by the front door. She said afterwards that she was really grateful I'd kept quiet all those years; that she respected me for it.'

Camilla and Douglas used the same restraint. Their two children didn't have their first babies until they were past thirty. Douglas says, 'They didn't finish their education until their late twenties, so there really hadn't been time before that to think about children. We weren't worried that we'd never have grandchildren, but we *did* dream about it – doesn't every parent? Having a family is a wonderful thing.' Camilla says: 'We knew they wanted babies – we just tried to be patient. Our children are healthy, so I wasn't concerned there would be problems but, as Douglas says, we did dream. We'd find ourselves gazing in baby shop windows and having a wander round Mothercare, just looking at all the things you can buy – expecting to be happy. Watching other grandparents and seeing how much love there was, I kept thinking – I'd like it soon, I hope it will be soon. And suddenly it was there. It's a maturing thing . . .'

Douglas and Camilla trusted that their children wanted babies, but they were wise enough to leave the subject in the background. Sometimes starting a family isn't a simple matter of choice. When couples can't have a baby it can be a tragedy for everyone. Polly's daughter Mia tried for years.

It was heartbreaking. All Mia had ever wanted from the age of three was babies. She and her husband Calum tried and tried but after seven years and two miscarriages they decided to go for IVF treatment.

I managed to help them to pay for some of the IVF – it wasn't available on the NHS where they live and they couldn't have afforded it on their own. I was there for her all the way through four attempts, but they failed. It was tragic – each time we'd get our hopes up and each time we'd be knocked back. I'd cry but I didn't show it, not in front of Mia.

The fourth attempt worked for a few months and Mia was ecstatic. She and Calum even named the babies and went out shopping for loads of clothes and baby equipment. They knew it wasn't sensible, but they couldn't help themselves. They were counting the minutes – but then she lost the babies. It emerged Mia couldn't carry to term. I'd have carried one for her myself if I'd been menstruating. If your child wants a baby, you'll do anything to help, won't you?

It all took years, and my outgoing, cheerful daughter

became withdrawn, deeply unhappy. The whole thing had a disastrous effect on her health. In the end I told her I thought enough was enough. IVF is cripplingly expensive and on top of everything else they'd got into debt – the whole thing was blighting their life. Mia and Calum agreed. Since then they've tried to adopt but haven't been lucky – it's very, very difficult to adopt in Britain these days.

It's a terrible deprivation for Mia – she was born to be a mother. And it's dreadful for me as well. I lost a child myself when I was young and it's left a baby-shaped hole in me. I'll never resign myself to not being a grandmother.

Despite what Polly says, she clearly *has* come to terms with her daughter's situation. She's faced facts and advised Mia to put the struggle behind her because it's best for her, even though she knows what a hard choice it's been. No mother could do more.

For some couples IVF works out more happily. After trying for ten years, Nancy and Gordon were fortunate enough to have twin boys at their first IVF attempt. Gordon's parents, Isabelle and Charlie, were thrilled. Charlie explained: 'We'd more or less given up on being grandparents. Our other son Frank doesn't want kids. His wife, Myra, is into her career and he's not bothered. So then when it all came right for Nancy we were over the moon. It was amazing when they told us – we all cried our eyes out. Just like one of those corny movies; not a dry eye in the house. And it's been amazing. Oliver and Robin are three now and we couldn't love them more. They're a big bonus – the grandchildren we never expected to have. Isabelle shops her head off and knits sweaters like there's no tomorrow, and I'm trying to teach them to swim the crawl. It's a bit of a challenge but I love it!' Isabelle and Charlie are enjoying every moment of their grandsons, and it's especially wonderful for them because they had no thoughts of grandchildren at all.

Francine's son Martin is four years younger than his wife, Jackie. When Jackie turned thirty, Francine started wondering. 'The clock was ticking for Jackie – but of course Martin is still comparatively young, so I kept quiet. I thought she was probably struggling with their age difference a bit. I didn't worry too much; I thought if it happened it would be great, but when it did my reaction made me think I must have been getting broody. Pia is eleven months now and super. Being a grandma is an OK label.' What Francine has realised is that when grandchildren arrive they have a way of changing your attitude in seconds, even more dramatically then when your own children were born. It's unique because this time round it's somehow bittersweet.

Perhaps this is because you know you'll only be there for a small part of their lives, or because you love them as much as your children but they aren't *yours* in the same way, or because they come to you so many years later, and now you know how fleeting and special babyhood and childhood actually are. Maybe it's gratitude at being given a second chance with hindsight. Or perhaps it's a combination of all those things. Whatever it is, it's an epiphany, a realisation that the world goes on, and that you're experiencing an amazing and wonderful new set of feelings.

Madeleine is a grandmother of ten. Whenever or however your grandchildren arrive, her words sum it up: 'When I held my grandson in my arms I thought – this is what my whole life has been building up to. It's hard to be a parent, but it's easy to be a grandparent.'

TALKING TO YOUR CHILDREN

It's Best Not to Say:

When are you going to give us grandchildren?
You're setting up expectations.

It's time you started thinking about babies.
You're telling them what to do.

The clock's ticking.
You're putting pressure on.

You'll be too old soon.
You might worry them.

You'll regret it if you leave it too late.
You're lecturing them.

Couples without children become self-centred.
You're hinting they are.

You're being selfish.
They wouldn't be doing it for you.

It's not fair to disappoint us.
Now you're being selfish.

Who'll look after you when you're old?
If they aren't worrying about that – you shouldn't be.

It's OK to Say – Once:

If you ever feel like having kids we'll be thrilled.

THINGS TO TELL YOURSELF

This isn't about *you* – however much you might feel it is.
It's not actually your business – however much you might
   think it is.
What's right for you might not be right for them.
Your children have more going on in their lives and relation-
   ship than you know. They don't tell you everything.
What you felt at that age might not be what they feel now.

2
Wall-to-Wall Baby

There are times in ordinary, everyday life which can be
described as scary: our first day at school; the first time we
drive a car; walking into a new job or major relationship.
They're like stepping off the end of the pier into freezing
water – exciting, even wonderful – but they take your breath
away. Becoming a parent probably falls into that category for
most of us: the moment when the drama, excitement and
trauma of the birth is over, the doctors and other experts
have left us to it, and suddenly it hits us – we're parents! Here
we are alone with this little life, completely responsible for

its well-being, comfort, happiness – survival. Remember that feeling?

Whether it's our first baby, or fourth, it's not just a big moment, it's huge. We look down at this helpless child and vow we'll do everything within our power to give it a marvellous life: we'll love, protect and nurture it for all time. And we intend to do it *our* way. *We* won't make the same mistakes our parents made. No, we'll redefine the whole meaning of good parenting. What happens next is chaos. It doesn't matter how many children you already have, how much you know, how confident you feel, the chaos comes just the same.

As grandparents we understand what's awaiting our children – these brand new parents who have just thrown off their L-plates – the strangeness, the mind-boggling challenges, the seemingly unassailable mountains of work. We know nothing will ever be the same again for them; that someone else's needs now come first and always will. Within an incredibly short space of time what they regard as normal will be whipped into the past – and the here and now is strange uncharted territory. Unfamiliar routines, the need to acquire new skills instantly, juggle tasks, absorb a mountain of often conflicting information and advice – it all hits them at once like a bucketful of sand in the face.

If they already have children, baby basics will hold no fear, but fitting them into an already packed routine is a challenge. Not just the physical hours-in-a-day thing, but the emotional fallout: sibling displacement, jealousy . . . New parents will be overwrought, maybe tetchy – and that's before the sleepless nights have begun to bite. Oh yes, chaos reigns.

Wall-to-wall baby – while it's happening it can feel like for ever, although it doesn't last for more than a few weeks. But those first weeks of a baby's life is a unique time and all the more precious because it's so brief. With all our experience, we can help our children not only to cope practically and emotionally, but to *enjoy* it. We can enable them to get the very most out of it, make it easy for them in whatever ways they find acceptable, so that they look back on it with affection, as a period when they drew close to their new child and each other – and forged deeper bonds with their parents.

Offering to Help

It's one thing to know our children could do with some help; it's quite another to get them to accept it. The need of new parents to do everything themselves, to be hands-on, not bystanders, is instinctive, primeval. How do you even broach the subject?

Remember how you felt when your first baby was born. Think back and try to recapture the tremendous sense of pride bordering on ownership, and let that give you some clues as to how to approach it.

When They Live Near You

If you live nearby, you might suggest popping in every day or so to do a few chores or get some shopping. You could just say, 'Look, I know you'll be busy with the baby – if I drop in regularly at a time that suits you, you can tell me what you'd like me to do.' Suggest practical ways to help rather than offer to take over the baby care itself. Offer to take washing and ironing away with you instead of spending hours at their home; they might want to be left together in peace to bond as a family.

Roger and Natalie didn't think of that when their daughter Val's son was born. Roger says:

When Val and Roddy had little Nathan we thought, great, Natalie had just retired and she could move in with them for a couple of weeks and give them a lovely rest. We mentioned it about a month before he was born and Val looked really embarrassed. She said, 'But I don't want you to, Mum. It's all right – we'll be fine. Come and see us though.' I could see Natalie was a bit hurt, but afterwards we thought about it and decided if that's what Val and Roddy wanted then that's what we'd do. So we made a list of things that would help to make them comfortable without intruding, and gave it to Val. She leapt at all of them – things like filling their freezer with home-made meals, doing a twice-weekly supermarket run, collecting the dirty washing every two days and bringing it back clean, mowing the lawn and weeding (those were my jobs!). It all went like a dream. Val and Roddy had all the help they needed and we benefited too. We got to see a lot of Nathan, because when we were there, everything was so relaxed.

It's a good idea to talk things over with your children well before the birth. That way there's time to plan. It might also prevent you from having expectations that won't be fulfilled. Val's refusal made Natalie and Roger realise that what was happening wasn't about *them* – it was about their daughter and her partner. It sounds obvious, but in fact it can be hard to remember because as grandparents you feel that big tug – a child who's not yours but is still, somehow, such a big part of you. Instinct can kick in and it's very easy to find yourself in the middle of the road directing the traffic when your children really need you to be picking up the litter on the pavement. It can be hard to take a back seat, but if that's what your children need, then you'll want to support them. It doesn't mean they don't love you. They're depending on you to be there for them, even if it's in the background.

The In-Law Factor

If you're looking for clues as to how to help (and how not to), it can be useful to remember how your parents and parents-in-law acted in your day. Sybil visited her daughter Lydia every day after her granddaughter, Pippa, was born. 'I'd walk the dog round to Lydia's. I suppose I assumed she wouldn't mind, but I was very careful, because I remember very well that when Lydia was born, my mother-in-law took over completely. The very first time we ever took her for a walk – brand new baby, brand new pram – I so wanted to push her myself, but my mother-in-law did it and I walked alongside. I've never forgotten how much I minded. I wouldn't ever have spoilt it for Lydia like that.'

No doubt Sybil's mother-in-law thought she was being helpful – that she knew best; she didn't try to imagine or remember how it felt to be a proud new mum. And in those days, of course, Sybil wouldn't have criticised her mother-in-law.

In fact, mothers-in-law are a whole separate ball game. The concept of total politeness and unquestioning subservience to our elders has mellowed into a more healthy equality but, still, constraints exist. However close you are to your daughter-in-law, she's likely to be closer to her own mother – it's natural. And however close she is to you, she's not your child, and she'll feel that. So there are limits. Depending on your relationship these might be slight, but they exist. They're there for fathers-in-law too, of course, but in the hormone-infested post-birth jungle, it tends to be the female who runs the risks.

When Keiran's wife, Fay, was pregnant, his mother, Kim,

asked her if she'd like her to come and look after them and
the baby after the birth. 'I thought she'd be pleased. Her own
mum is on the other side of the country and has a job, so I
just thought it would be easier for me. We'd always got on
well. She turned me down flat, saying her mum would be
coming. Fair enough, but her tone implied "Who do you
think you are?" I backed right off – I was annoyed. They'd
asked me to help them a lot when they'd moved into their
new flat. I was good enough for a bit of labouring, but not
when it came to babies. I learned my lesson and know my
place now.'

Kim is hurt because she feels she's been relegated to
second place. And in a way she's right, because the baby is
as much her son's as Fay's, and she wants to be involved. But
the biological link between mother and daughter is strong
in situations like this, and it's possible that Fay didn't mean
to hurt Kim at all. It would be better for Kim to give Fay
the benefit of the doubt and not allow a rift to develop over
something that is, after all, over within a couple of months.
She has the whole of the rest of her life to get to know and
love her grandson.

When You Live a Long Way Away

If you don't live near your children, it can be much harder
to give sustained help, because that involves staying in their
house. Jade and Ellis's daughter Lindy has lived abroad for
most of her married life. Jade says: 'I've gone to stay when
each child was born. I'm very close to my daughter but I
always wait to be invited. It's a happy time, but there's nothing
like staying with your son-in-law and grandchildren to get to
know their little foibles! It's a wonderful way to draw closer
because things become routine – natural – rather than the
excitement of a quick visit.' Jade and her daughter have a

good relationship that hasn't been weakened by living at a distance, and those post-baby stays are very important to both of them.

Ginny has a different view. Her parents live at the other end of the country, while her husband Alan's are round the corner. When her first baby was born, her mother and father came for a week, but Ginny didn't let them stay with her. 'I packed them off to stay at my in-laws. In retrospect, it was maybe a wee bit hurtful, but I wanted it to be just us. Mum didn't say anything about it and of course I saw them every day. When they went back home, Alan's mum came and went a bit to help. She was keen not to be on top of us.' Ginny probably regrets it now. With hindsight she feels she was perhaps a little selfish, not so much in wanting to be on her own with her new family – that's understandable – but in the way that she handled it. If she'd planned it and discussed it with her mother beforehand she might have avoided hurting her.

A lot of visitors just after the birth *can* become a bit overwhelming. Millie and Jason lived two hundred miles from both sets of parents. Millie says:

When Eloise was born, Jason's parents brought my mum on the day I came out of hospital. They were just going to stay for the day and then leave Mum with us for a week.

Jason and I got home with Eloise before everyone arrived and it was all calm and peaceful – for about five minutes. Then Eloise started yelling, a policeman arrived at the door to take a statement from Jason about a motorway accident he'd witnessed the week before, and the grandparents walked into the middle of it all, talking and fussing round the baby. It was a madhouse. I just stood looking round in a complete daze, and then my father-in-law quietly took my hand and walked me out of the flat and into the pub next door. He bought me a big glass of orange juice and said, 'Get that down you, it will do you good.' He told me not to worry – my mum and Jason's were experts and to let them get on with it; that I needed some peace and quiet, and they wouldn't miss me.

He was right, too. Jason joined us and we just relaxed for twenty minutes and then went back to the fray. I don't think the two mums had noticed we'd gone!

It probably seemed like good sense to have everyone travel together to take Millie's mother for her stay, and to give Jason's parents a chance to see the baby, but it was all too much at once for Millie. Where possible it's better to drip-feed visitors for everyone's sake, including the baby's.

When Avril's daughter Patty was having her first baby, she asked her mother to stay for a week.

Patty said would I go on the day she came out of hospital. She asked as though it was a big favour because she knew I'd have to take a week off work. But, of course, it wasn't a favour, it was a gift! And it was marvellous – we mostly just hung out together. She'd feed Jasmine, then sleep when she was down, while I got on with the chores. The rest of the time we'd chat, or take the baby for a walk, and in the evenings Patty would sit in the kitchen with me while I was cooking.

It was all very calm and low-key. My son-in-law Danny was at home too, but I don't think either of them felt I was intruding on their lives, although I did try to give them some space – I'd go and read in my room in the evening. To be frank it was good to put my feet up for a bit!

I got a lot of hands-on time with Jasmine too – my

daughter was very generous. It wouldn't have occurred to her to keep all the good stuff to herself, though I would have understood if she had. It was lovely – a very special time. Patty and I have always been close, and it just seemed natural to do it this way. I'm lucky.

Avril took the strain so all Patty had to do was enjoy her baby, and she had someone on hand to share all the mini-thrills that come in the first week of a baby's life – no detail is too small to be discussed, from the similarity with your grandfather's ears, to both your obstetric histories – it's a baby fest.

Avril's right – she *is* lucky that she and her daughter are so relaxed together and enjoy each other's company. Patty remembers:

Mum arrived straight from work at about 2 p.m., and I said, 'Here's the baby – I'm going to bed!' After being up the previous two nights I was absolutely tired out and I knew Mum wouldn't mind. Having a new baby is so intense you can get to the end of your tether. It was wonderful to be able to leave the newby with someone I could trust completely, and escape for a sleep. Mum knew what she was doing and, in any case, could have woken me if she'd needed to. It was such a relief.

Dad came that evening and held Jasmine while Mum cooked dinner for us all. It was perfect. That week I was up every night with Jasmine, who didn't sleep well, but during the day I got lots of rest because Mum had the chores and everything under control. So much so that Danny went back to work! We decided he could take the time off after Mum had gone home, when Jasmine would be bit more settled.

It worked well because it just set us off on the right track and made Jasmine's first week easy. When my second daughter was born I wanted Mum to do the same thing, but she couldn't because she had a flap on at work. We were both disappointed. I can't understand why anyone wouldn't want their mum to do this for them.

Not everyone feels the same as Avril and Patty. Diane loves her mother, but she didn't fancy the idea of her staying for a week. 'Mum's really chilled and doesn't get het up about things, but she only stayed a couple of days when my eldest, Edward, was born. She was helpful and it was great, but I couldn't have stood her for long. It's not her, it's me – I like my own space.'

If you want to suggest staying after the birth, how you play it will depend on your relationship with your daughter or daughter-in-law. It's worth bringing it up. Just don't take it personally if they say no. Erica has gone to stay for the birth of all her seven grandchildren – her daughters' and her son's. 'They've always asked me and I've been delighted to go. It's wonderful to be wanted in that way and to be able to help. My younger daughter lives a continent away and I went out for both her children's births. It's a privilege. I'm so happy I was able to do it for them.'

However you end up helping, a little or a lot, it's a marvellous opportunity to get closer to your children than you've ever been. In fact, the whole experience can show you new sides of each other, as Jan found when her daughter Catriona had her first baby, Alastair. 'Somehow we'd never imagined Catriona as a mother – she was always the career girl in our heads. But she was wonderful with Alastair – very tender and loving. It brought a lump to my throat to see it.'

It can heal wounds too. Roberta and her father, John,

hadn't seen much of each other since her parents' divorce when she was five.

When Harvey was born I phoned Dad to let him know – more because I thought I should than anything else – but he asked if he could see the baby. I wasn't all that keen, but I said yes, as long as he didn't come round when Mum was here.

He was great. Harvey took to him right from the start, and Dad was so good and funny with him. It kind of reminded me how he'd been with me when I was little. I'd forgotten in all those years without him. He'd change Harvey's nappy, give him a bottle and do loads of chores so I could get my head down while Harvey was asleep – he was as good as Mum! *And* he mended a leaky pipe and fixed a tile on the roof. He's right back in my life now and I'm determined he's going to stay in Harvey's.

Harvey was the way back for Roberta and John. Babies can work, if not actual magic, then wonders, if you treat their arrival as an opportunity to reflect on the way your life is, and how it could be.

Second Babies and Beyond

Help can be much more acceptable when subsequent babies come along because it's the siblings who need looking after. Lyn had her mother-in-law, Hermione, lined up to collect her daughter, Josie, when she went into labour. 'It was all fixed, but when my husband phoned Hermione, she said no, she was too busy to come straight away. I had to wait until she arrived before I could go to the hospital. I know she has a job, but she'd told me not to worry, she'd be there when it happened. I was cross. It just shows you can't rely on anyone.' Hermione probably didn't intend to let Lyn down – and in fact she didn't in the end, but it's better to have a fall-back position if there's a chance that circumstances might change. Emotions tend to run high and upsets can easily occur.

Taking care of your grandchildren while the new baby is being born is a key role. You're a familiar, solid point in what can be an unnerving situation for a young child. When Hetty and Walter's daughter Mitzi had her third baby, they were on alert to fetch the elder two as soon as Mitzi went into labour. Walter says:

> It was all carefully planned. We live about an hour away but traffic can triple that time, so the arrangement was that when Mitzi began her contractions, she'd phone us straight away and we'd go and collect our two granddaughters to stay with us for a couple of nights, until she came back home with the baby.
>
> In fact, Mitzi and William were so relaxed they didn't tell us until she was quite far on in labour. Then there was a long hold-up on the motorway. By the time we got there she was doing her breathing lying over one of those huge balls, and the contractions were only three minutes apart. *They* were still perfectly calm, but the girls were getting rather excited. Things were moving fast! We literally shoved Mitzi and William out of the door, scooped up the kids and left.
>
> They were six and four and well used to staying with us on their own, but that time they behaved like little monsters. They wet their knickers, fought, shrieked and bit lumps out of each other – it was like having two different children in the house. Of course it was because of the baby. We weren't actually cross, but we had to be very firm

with them or they'd have killed each other! Eventually they calmed down.

Walter and Hetty realised what their granddaughters were going through. However much they know they're loved, however secure children are, they're still going to feel a bit worried and anxious – their world is about to be invaded by a stranger. One reaction to this uncertainty can be to go back to baby ways themselves – making a fuss, demanding attention. William and Hetty's response was to treat them exactly as they always did: to be a fixed and normal point in their universe. They'd had plenty of practice at being parents and grandparents. Moira wasn't so experienced.

When my daughter-in-law Kayleigh had her second baby she asked me if I'd take my grandson Darrel for a few days. Of course I said yes – her own mum lived in Australia and was coming later in the year for six weeks.

Darrel was under two and a real handful at the best of times, but that week he was appalling. I'd always thought Kayleigh and my son let him get away with murder, but he was completely uncontrollable. He wouldn't eat, he wandered around half the night, and when he *was* in bed he'd be crying. He'd never stayed with me on his own before and, frankly, I didn't know how to handle him. If my husband had been alive we might have managed better, but it was just me. I worried myself to death and I think Darrel sensed it and just rampaged. I never told his parents. When they asked how he'd been I just said 'fine', but I was absolutely exhausted and glad to see the back of him! I didn't offer to have him again for a while.

Darrel was having to cope with the thought of having a

baby sibling – and at eighteen months he was still more or less a baby himself – he also had to do it on his own, while his mum and dad disappeared to produce the new baby he probably wasn't sure he wanted anyway. No wonder he kicked up . . .

Involving Siblings

It makes sense to have the other children to stay with you for the birth, because it leaves the parents free to concentrate on the job in hand. But looked at from the child's point of view, it can seem as though their parents are abandoning them to focus on a strange creature who hasn't even arrived yet – very scary. This highlights how important it is to explain to children just what's going to happen and why. Parents and grandparents can minimise this feeling if they sit down with the child and talk through the plans. Make it an adventure, a treat – you're going to be coming for a special short holiday and we're going to do X and Y and then we'll take you home to meet your new baby, so you can help your mum and dad look after him/her. It's important *they're* the centre of attention so they don't feel they're being banished.

It can help too, to have them to stay with you on their own before the event. If they haven't already, try to achieve it at least once in the run up to the birth so you're all old hands.

Of course the opposite can also be true. Your children might prefer you to go and stay with your grandchildren while the baby's born. This has the advantage of keeping them in their familiar environment and at the centre of things – but you need to be sure that they *are* at the centre of things when the baby actually arrives, along with the inevitable stream of adoring visitors. Your role can be to make that happen.

Pru's son Gregory and his partner, Holly, had their second baby when their daughter, Freya, was four.

Holly's own parents are dead, and she asked us to stay with

them for a few days so that Freya could still go to pre-school in the mornings. It seemed like a good idea to keep to her routine, but the house was like a railway station. Holly has loads of relatives and they were there at all hours. My husband, Ralph, would fetch Freya from school and she'd walk into this morass of people all passing the baby round. They hardly noticed Freya except to ask how she liked her little brother. What a stupid question! As far as Freya was concerned he was already a pain in the neck.

Ralph and I didn't want her to be lonely among all these people, so we'd cook her a 'special' lunch every day, something no one else was having. We'd eat with her, and then have a little activity planned for the three of us to do together – nothing fancy, just something like drawing pictures or making chocolate brownies. Her face would light up – 'What are we doing today, Nana?'

Even when children are in their own house, it helps to explain, so that they understand what's going on around them. With the best will in the world, new parents are going to be a bit preoccupied, so by concentrating on the children, you'll involve them: plan and wrap a present together for the baby (not forgetting a little something for *them* too), maybe blow up some balloons. Try to get the children out of the house sometimes, to the park, the shops, the library – anywhere out of earshot of all the cooing and endless talk that isn't directed at *them*. And try not to be guilty of this yourself. Imagine how it feels to lose your place in your family – your mother and father, your grandmas and granddads, were yours and yours alone, and now all everyone talks about or to, is this stranger who just lies there and sleeps, and then wakes and cries, and everyone rushes up and makes a fuss. (It's tempting to try a little crying yourself . . .)

You could take the baby out with you and let them push the pram – that will have the double benefit of giving the child an important role and giving the new mother a much-needed break. Just don't talk about the baby all the time you're out. Another way grandparents can help siblings feel wanted is to tell stories of when *their* mum or dad was born. This makes what's happening seem less cataclysmic – it's happened before, and to the most important people in their lives – their parents.

When Things Go Wrong

Of course everyone hopes for a safe, simple, straightforward birth – but that doesn't always happen. And when things do go wrong, whether seriously or in relatively minor ways, it's worrying for everyone involved. In this kind of crisis your children need you to be flexible and accommodating, calm and, above all, *there* for them to lean on. You're supporting them emotionally, as well as giving them the practical back-up that will leave them free to deal with problems as they arise.

Janice and Patrick did this for their son Grant and his wife, Kay. Patrick recalls: 'Kay was admitted to hospital nine weeks early with suspected pre-eclampsia. It turned out not to be that, but little Frank was put in an incubator, and he and Kay stayed in hospital for ten days. We live just down the road from them, so Janice would pop round to look after Grant, cook his meals and so on. He was in a mad panic trying to decorate the baby's room – of course they hadn't thought they'd need to finish it so soon.' Janice says:

They're not particularly house-proud, but what with the decorating, shampooing the carpets, and the fact that Grant was trying to spend as much time as possible at the hospital with Kay, the place was pretty untidy. I didn't clear up too much though – after all it's their house. What we did do was tell people to phone us for news of Kay and Frank, rather than hassling Grant. He had enough on his plate.

When they came out of hospital, Kay was tired and not very well, so I became the caterer – they'd come round and eat with us in the evenings. They'd just turn up without warning and go straight to the fridge. I've always got food, and it was nice that they felt they could.

Patrick adds: 'Frank's doing fine now, but those first few weeks were worrying for all of us. He was so small. They looked up everything in a book. It's natural under the circumstances, but I wanted to tear it to bits! Grant dotes on the baby and was always thinking there was something wrong with him. I kept saying, "He's *OK*." I remember Frank was outside in his pram one hot day and he was sweating. Grant took his temperature about five times, put him in a cool bath and was on the phone to Janice straight away.' Patrick and Janice could see what needed doing to help their family. They were reassuring, took up the slack and made themselves available.

A simple, practical hand may be all that's needed, but sometimes it's more complicated than that. When Adam and Caroline's daughter-in-law was pregnant she was prescribed complete bed rest. Caroline says:

Colette had had two sons, then several miscarriages, so this time the doctors were concerned. They told her she had to stay in bed for three months, which obviously meant she wouldn't be able to look after the children. I couldn't take all that time away from home so I offered to have the boys to stay with us. Colette wouldn't do it, she wouldn't be parted from them for so long and I could see why. I said, 'OK, all three of you come here, you can rest completely and *I'll* look after the children.' For me, family is the most important thing in the world.

Our son Barney came down at weekends, and the local school here agreed to have our grandsons for a term. It worked out very well. They settled beautifully and seemed to enjoy themselves. Adam and I loved having them, and their mother was able to stay in bed. She went home a month before her daughter was born, and I went with her to look after her then.

Caroline is a busy woman with a lot of commitments, but although these meant she couldn't spend three months away, she was prepared to fit herself round her family. Being flexible can work wonders.

However, nothing can prepare you for some situations. Heather's presence was essential to her daughter Amy whose partner, Henry, died two months before her daughter was born.

The shock was appalling, but Amy kept on working until five days before the baby arrived. It was good for her to have something to keep her occupied. I only live six miles away, and I went to stay and was with her for Chloe's birth – I took Henry's place. After four days I went home, but for a couple of weeks I drove back every evening to spend the night there. I'd do the 2 a.m. feed so Amy could get some sleep.

And of course, on top of her grief, there were the usual new baby things – she wanted to breastfeed and had trouble latching on, for example. But then there were problems we'd never have anticipated. I was helping her with all the jobs she'd have done with Henry like registering the birth, and we found she couldn't put Henry's name down as the father on the certificate because they hadn't been married and he'd died before the baby was born. She had to prove he was the father. They took DNA samples and asked Amy all sorts of questions, like how many men she'd slept with; it was all awful for her, but she was superb. Of course she's got Henry's name on the birth certificate now, but the whole process was a terrible strain after what she'd gone through. We were with her for all of it.

Amy needed her mother on all sorts of levels at a time when she was incredibly lonely and insecure. Heather gave her daughter courage just by being strong for her, in her corner, on her side.

There are laws governing the claiming of paternity in these circumstances. Initially, the mother has to register the child in her own name and then put in a petition to the local court for a change of name. The judge will order a pre-trial hearing at which she will be questioned (this may involve stating her sexual partners) and witness' statements read. The law may vary in details and procedure between England, Wales, Scotland and Northern Ireland, so contact your local register office. (See pages 254–5 for useful addresses.)

When the parents aren't married, inheritance can be an issue too, if, for example, there's no will and the father dies before the baby is born. Karen's common-law partner, Ned, died five months before their son was born and her mother, Charlotte, is convinced that couples need to understand the implications: 'Ned hadn't made a will – it didn't occur to him – young people think they'll live for ever, don't they? But when he died of a heart attack he left Karen in real financial difficulties.'

The laws on intestacy for spouses and civil partners aren't the same as for common-law partners, and again they might also vary regionally. (See pages 254–5 for useful addresses.)

Calming the Storms

Any new mother is going to be tired and emotional. Pregnancy and birth isn't an illness but it isn't exactly a cake-walk either. The birth might have been easy – but define *easy*. Contractions, episiotomies, stitches and needles, bruising, sore nipples, feelings of insecurity and stress – it's a full-on experience and it takes a lot out of them. Grandmothers will remember their own experience vividly. They say the memory of contractions fades, and maybe it does, but the other discomforts tend to remain in a woman's data banks.

There can be a feeling of anticlimax about it, too. Even though she's got the star prize and brought it home under her arm, the build-up to birth is so big that it's possible to feel a bit 'morning after the awards dinner' – as though the excitement's over. This feeling doesn't last, but from the relative glamour of the birth (yes, glamour, because it's all happening round *her*) suddenly the new mother looks at herself and sees a wreck. Post-birth beauty might shine from within but a new mother won't be winning any prizes for grooming. Bags under her eyes, wrecked hair she doesn't have time to wash, T-shirt stiff with dried milk and a tummy resembling a deflating hot-air balloon – she'll be feeling less than appealing.

And then she looks at the devastation of her home: heaps of baby clothes on the chairs, more baby clothes drying everywhere, open packs of nappies, changing mat, wipes, cream, a tangle of pushchair, cot, stuffed toys – and it's all over the house . . . does she actually *live* here?

Given all this, it's quite likely that the new mum will have at least one tantrum during the first few weeks – and you might find yourself on the receiving end of it. Try not to rise to it: remember you're not really the target. In a way it's a compliment; she's just venting her insecurity and feels safe to do it with you.

And it's not just the mother – the father might not have swollen milk glands, but he's going through his own epiphany. His blooming partner of a few hours ago has turned into this stranger with a whole new set of duties that seem to have nothing to do with him. It's been said (by men) that birth is a totally female thing, and you can see what they mean. It's possible for a new father to feel excluded, displaced, un-necessary – unwanted even.

When Diana and Mathew had their twins, Mathew's mother, Cherie, went round every day to lend a hand.

I could see things were getting on top of them. I mean, a single baby when it's brand new seems to fill all the avail-able time you have. You get it down to sleep and it takes you at least until the next feed to catch up with everything else. Imagine what it's like with twins! Once or twice when I was there they had a little spat – not much, just a bit of under the breath hissing, a slammed door. Mathew flounced out a couple of times and left my daughter-in-law having a weep.

I cuddled her, shampooed her hair and gave it a blow dry. Another time I ran her a deep bath and told her to stay in it until it cooled. I said the twins weren't the only ones who benefited from a nice warm soak.

I had a quiet word with my son, too. I said, 'Look, love, you can flounce out, but Diana can't leave the babies, can she? You have to do this together. No one's an expert in the first five minutes, but by the time the twins are a year old you'll be writing manuals.' We had a laugh about it. It seemed to work and they calmed down. And naturally things got easier over the next two or three weeks, anyway. They call me Oprah, now!

Of course Diana and Mathew were stressed. New parents want to do everything right – to be perfect – and that's a lot of pressure.

Baby Blues and Post-Natal Depression (PND)

For about half of new mothers, it goes further and they get a bout of baby blues. No one really knows what causes this, although many doctors believe it's the result of the cocktail of hormones fizzing round a woman's body after giving birth. It can start a couple of days after the birth with flashes of irritability, tearfulness and tiredness and usually disappears within a few days of its own accord, but it's still a form of depression, and while it's happening the mother can feel miserably unhappy and unwell. It's worth keeping an eye on things to check that it gradually wears off because it could, in some cases, lead to PND, even if it isn't itself an early stage of PND.

It might seem unlikely that your daughter or daughter-in-law will suffer from PND, but it's more common than people think. It affects one in ten women and can appear within the first few weeks, or take several months to become noticeable, which can make it difficult to diagnose; it's a serious illness and needs medical attention.

When Amanda's son James was born she asked her mother, Nicole, to stay for a week.

Mum said, 'Ooh yes!' She was as pleased as Punch, but of course I wanted her. I mean, I didn't know anything about babies. And I wasn't very well. I had mastitis and internal infections, and so Mum stayed on for a while. I felt rotten, weepy and low, and Mum was amazing. I couldn't have coped without her. I absolutely dreaded her going home. It got worse and worse, and she offered to stay on with us, but we didn't really have the space. We were renovating the house, and, anyway, she needed to get back to Dad. So she went home and I struggled on.

I was on maternity leave, and trying to decide whether or not to stop working and stay at home with James. I couldn't bear the thought of anyone else looking after him, but Paul had started his own business and I was earning more than him.

When James was six months old, I finally decided I wouldn't go back to work, but then I started to feel even worse. With no job, I felt like a second-class citizen − as though my life had ended. The house was a mess; I was worried about Paul's business and our finances − it was all a nightmare. My whole life had been turned upside down. I was constantly in tears over the most stupid things. Paul was very sympathetic, but I was so insecure − I thought no one else had ever felt like this before. I'd phone Mum all the time and cry. She'd come to stay sometimes − if she could have come to live I'd have jumped at it. My in-laws would offer to take James for a few hours so I could have some rest, and Mum would say, let them help, let them do it. I did, but even though they were fantastic, I hated leaving him with *anyone*. Here was this baby who I felt had ruined my life, yet he was the most important thing in it − I was incredibly protective.

Each month I got worse and finally Mum persuaded me

to see my doctor. He diagnosed post-natal depression, and with treatment it eventually got better.

PND can occur for a lot of reasons, and often it's a combination of several factors rather than one single cause. (See pages 255–6 for further information.) But depression of any kind is a lonely and isolating condition. Nicole was a lifeline for Amanda – just knowing her mother was a phone call away made all the difference to her. Nicole realised her daughter needed medical help and encouraged her to get it.

It's easy for the mother to convince herself that what she's feeling is normal – tired, tearful, irritable – but PND goes way beyond this. Common symptoms include feeling worthless and useless, an inability to sleep even when exhausted, loss of appetite, lethargy and lack of interest in anything, worrying all the time, panic attacks – classic symptoms of depression.

Women can be tempted to hide all this. They're ashamed of themselves because they think they 'ought' to be coping; that they should pull themselves together and get on with it; that there's nothing really wrong with them. So the longer it goes on and the worse it gets, the more they might try to conceal it. This is part of the illness too. If you think there might be something wrong, then have a talk with your children. Don't frighten them – you don't need to mention PND – just get them to describe how they feel, and listen. In fact, just talking to someone they can trust about how awful they feel can be an enormous help. Take as much of the practical daily strain as you can, and suggest they see their doctor, who'll take it from there if there's anything to pursue. The sooner PND is diagnosed, the better – and it *can* be treated.

It's possible that if you suffered from PND after one baby, you might develop it with subsequent ones. This happened to Hayley. 'I didn't get it so badly with my second or third child, but my mum did everything – she came to stay each time and was a tower of strength. When my son was born she even took him into her room every night so I could get some sleep. I don't know what I'd have done without her. With my third baby I was taking medication all the way through the pregnancy but I still needed help afterwards. I feel so guilty for not being 'there' to help with my own babies, and wish I could have enjoyed their babyhood more – but Mum was wonderful. I just wish she lived closer to us.' Hayley's mother understood what her daughter needed – unconditional love and support. Hayley shouldn't feel guilty about what happened – she couldn't help it any more that you can help catching flu. It wasn't her fault.

Imparting Your Wisdom

All new parents go through an enormous learning curve. *You* might feel like a world-class expert, but how did that happen? By hands-on learning and making your own mistakes. But perhaps they're not mistakes, just a different point of view . . .

Nerissa and Morgan's daughter Julia had her own ideas about new babies. Morgan says, 'Nerissa trod very lightly, but her instincts were all the other way. I could see her hovering, wanting to take over. She held back and said – would you like me to? There's a limit to how much you can interfere. Every generation has slightly different ways. When Julia was a baby we'd wrap her up firmly – that was what you did – but Julia let Barnabas just flop, somehow. I know Nerissa would have loved to wrap him, but she didn't!'

Nerissa did the right thing. The fact is, however much you

think you know, things change, medical advice alters and, unless you've been spending the last thirty years studying baby theory, you're going to be out of date. Research into sudden infant death syndrome has radically altered advice; a lot if it is diametrically different from our day. Babies are now put down to sleep on their backs not their fronts; Dr Spock's early diktat of an ambient temperature of over 80°F in a baby's bedroom is now considered far too hot; sleeping bags have replaced blankets; talcum powder, which was sprinkled around lavishly twenty years ago, is taboo. There are a million points that will have passed you by.

Beattie discovered this when her daughter Jean had her first baby. 'I would go over to visit her and we'd sit and chat. Jean would ask me about techniques in my day, the things I'd done with her, and I'd tell her, thinking – this is nice, she wants to learn. But then I started to realise there were lots of things she was planning to do differently. A couple of times, quite spontaneously, I said, "But that's daft, it makes much more sense to do it my way," and she got quite brusque. She was very dismissive – not rude, just not taking me seriously, as if I didn't know anything! After all it had been more than thirty years since she was born. "We know more now, Mum," she said. I felt quite put down.'

If your daughter or, more particularly, your daughter-in-law does this, don't be tempted to lecture. Tell her how you did it if she wants to know, but don't try to persuade her. For one thing it won't have any effect except to confirm you as a dinosaur, and for another, think how you hated it when *your* seniors pulled rank.

It's worth having a look at what's out there, filling yourself in – you might be surprised at what you don't know. And you can impress the pants off your children with your grasp of baby facts. (See pages 254–5.) Try not to criticise. A lot is expected of a new mother – in fact she expects it of herself – so sometimes just the idea of criticism, not even criticism itself, can be enough to cause a tiff. Especially if it comes from a mother-in-law.

Jocelyn got into that kind of trouble with her daughter-in-law Wanda. 'When my granddaughter Ella was born, I was cuddling her and I made a joke about how I'd run away with her. You know the sort of thing "*I'm* going to take care of you, sweetheart." I didn't mean anything, but Wanda was really off with me – wouldn't let me change her nappy or anything. I had to ask to hold her. In the end my son Howard put me straight. He said Wanda had panicked when I said that. She'd taken it seriously as a slight on her ability to cope. I explained it was the last thing I meant – I wasn't trying to put in a takeover bid! We get on fine, but I'm much more careful now. Wanda's not my daughter.' It's clear Jocelyn still thinks Wanda was silly to take it wrongly, but when you're inexperienced you're quite likely to over-react to little things. Your life is littered with tiny decisions, and they can seem overwhelming.

There may be other reasons for feeling stressed. Cheryl's mother, Fiona, went to stay for a weekend when her grandson was born.

They were living in France at the time because of her husband's job, but Cheryl had already lost two babies so he brought her back to their house in England for the birth, and we arrived the day after. Everything was fine, but Cheryl was very jumpy. It was, 'Don't touch the baby!' 'Wash your hands before you pick her up!' She was so fussy – fuss, fuss, fuss. I'd never seen her like that before. All routine went out of the window. I didn't take it personally – I knew it wasn't meant that way. I just took over the bottles and nappies and so on. It seemed natural to do it and Cheryl was pleased to let me. I left the mess though – it seemed more tactful. I saw a lot of little Marcus and got plenty of cuddles, but she was very possessive of him.

Fiona perfectly understands why her daughter was being so careful – if, like Cheryl, you've lost two babies, this one will be so precious you might well feel possessive – how could you help it? So Fiona didn't criticise, she just got on with the job. She knew Cheryl wanted her there.

If things seem to be getting emotional, then the best way to keep it calm is probably to hold your tongue, be low-key and get on with what needs doing. Your children will appreciate it, even though they might not show it at the time.

PEACEKEEPING

Don't

State your opinions as facts.

Say anything that begins 'In my day . . .'

Criticise an aspect of modern thinking your children have espoused – unless asked what you think, or you believe it's actively dangerous.

Breeze in and take over – anything.

Offer advice unasked.

Silently alter something they've done with or for the baby.

Do

Ask, 'What would you like me to do?'

Say, 'How would you like me to do . . . [whatever]?'

Suggest things like, 'Shall I make you a sandwich/cup of tea/ meal, do the washing-up, put a load of washing in, pop to the shops, run the vac round?'

Be encouraging, not critical, even by implication.

3

Do Grandparents Know Best?

This is the 64,000-dollar question. Parenthood is the biggest responsibility that most of us will undertake, yet we do it without qualifications – we come into it cold. There are plenty of books on how to be a parent but, essentially, it's on-the-job training. We have to trust our instincts, fly by the seat of our pants. Of course we make mistakes, but we learn from them.

So by the time our children have grown up, most of us believe we're pretty experienced – we've coped with their terrible twos, survived all the teenage angst and, eventually, watched them leave the nest. If we've come this far and they're still speaking to us, we're battle-hardened veterans. But do we know best about our grandchildren? That's another question entirely.

As a card-carrying member of the parental fraternity you might feel you do – you're a skilled professional; a powerhouse of knowledge; you've been there, done it, got the gold star. What's more, you've had a couple of decades to work out the kinks in what you did last time and develop a few choice theories of your own. You're the biz. Of course, you won't be thinking of yourself in quite those terms, just that you have the background to help your children – to smooth their path – and you're keen to do it.

From your children's point of view things might look a bit different. However much they love and respect you, however much or little they know, they want – no, *need* – to do things for themselves, and you could almost be seen as a threat to that. Remember when you were a child struggling to fly a kite or manipulate a yoyo, and some officious grown-up kept taking it off you to show you how to do it? 'I *know*' you'd say, and wait impatiently until they gave it back.

On one level, of course, we do know more than our children, because we've been parents for much longer than they have – but knowing more isn't necessarily the same as knowing better. That's partly because, in everything from conception onwards, expert opinion changes constantly, new discoveries are made, thinking alters. We might have been state-of-the-art in our own day, but we're definitely retro now. It's also because each family unit is unique; its dynamics don't exist in any other context. The relationship you have, or had, with your father isn't the same as the one your son has with you, or that *his* son has with him – not worse or better

– just different. How you dealt with your daughter isn't automatically the template for how your child should deal with his/hers. Just think of the baggage every generation carries around. We've all said of our own parents at some time, 'I'll never do/say/act that way with my children.' No doubt our children will have said the same about us . . . So while we might have vast stores of tried and tested knowledge, it isn't necessarily going to be a perfect fit to what's happening now, and some of it will be as defunct as the yellowing instruction leaflet for a 1970s tape recorder.

But then again, some of it will be immensely valuable: the common sense; the wisdom; the insight into human nature we've gained over our lifetime; the understanding and compassion, objectivity and self-knowledge we've acquired through dealing, not only with our family, but with people in general. Combine this with the marvel of hindsight, and we really do have a basket of goodies our children can dive into as they struggle to do their best for *their* children. As long as they can do the diving when they want to, not when *we* think they should.

So do we know best? The answer probably is, yes – *sometimes* – but it isn't always a good idea to say so.

And the truth is, that although we know this, we're not infallible or perfect. We might say that we won't, or don't, interfere, but we will – and we do. So the real question is – how do we get the balance right?

Saying Your Piece

Given that, with the best will in the world, we *are* going to stick our oar in from time to time, when do we do it? And how do we do it, without bringing about one of those unpleasant family arguments – or worse – creating distance between our children and ourselves and becoming the subject of a private conversation between them beginning 'I wish [your] mum/dad wouldn't . . .'

Deciding When to Pipe Up

This depends on how strongly you feel. There are sure to be plenty of small issues you'd like to chip in over, but it's probably better to let them pass. As you've lived through it all before, you're well placed to know which they are. You have the perspective to realise that many things, though they seem huge at the time, have no long-term effects, so they're really not worth getting upset about. They'll soon be totally irrelevant, and forgotten just as quickly. A row, on the other hand, might not be.

The decision is yours, of course, but, before you jump in with both feet, it's worth stopping to think about whether what's worrying you is only important in the short term. You want everything to be right for the grandchild you love, so it can be hard to hold back – especially if the child in question is still a baby. But be careful. Babies are a particularly emotive issue – one that seems to generate differences of opinion spontaneously. In fact, some debates have been raging for generations and will create pitfalls in any family pathway, if you let them.

Routine is one of these, it was dividing mothers and daughters two generations ago, and not just mothers, as Malcolm and Edith discovered. Malcolm recalls:

When our daughter's first baby was born she went in for a strict routine – and I mean strict. Everything had to be done by the clock. We thought they were making life hard for themselves, but we didn't say so. Then one day my daughter handed me my grandson and said, 'He's sleepy but he can't go down for another twelve minutes. Keep him awake for me.'

I looked at this droopy child, whose eyes kept closing and whose head was falling on my shoulder. 'Tickle his feet,' my daughter said. I thought it was cruel keeping him up like that – babies know when they need sleep, don't they? So I just handed him back and said, 'If you want to keep this child awake *you* can do it – I'm not.' I didn't say anything else – and neither did my daughter. Edith said later that if *she'd* done that there would have been ructions! There's something to be said for being a man.

If you do decide to bring up something like this, don't lose your temper or get heated. Just make your point quietly, without accusations. Malcolm didn't tell his daughter he thought it was cruel – he knew she was trying to do the best for her baby. He just said he wasn't going to do what she asked, which meant that there was nothing to argue or get defensive about.

Morris and Claudia have several grandchildren, and firm rules on when to speak their mind. Claudia says: 'We never comment on things like the way our children are teaching table manners, for example, although we're not always happy with it! Or the way they dress them – things like that. We don't see that as our job. But if it's something very important then we will say it – once. They've been discussing the possibility of boarding school. Now *that's* a big thing and we have a view. We don't approve of it, and our children know that. They're well aware of what we think and why, so there's no point in going on about it.'

This is wise of them. They've discussed it with their children without falling out, or trying to strong-arm them, so their views are more likely to be taken into consideration when they make their decision – but it will be *their* decision.

Ted and Candy don't agree with their son Declan about vaccinations – and they felt this was sufficiently important to raise. Ted says:

> Dec and his wife, Emily, have got it into their heads that vaccinations are dangerous, and they told us our grand-daughter Katie won't be having them. They mentioned it in passing but we were horrified. What on earth do they think they're playing at? Take measles – they don't realise the permanent damage it can do to a child, so they don't under-stand the implications – they have no experience of it, and that's thanks to *us* taking responsibility when *they* were little. We just let go and gave them a real rollicking for being irre-sponsible. We said they were falling for the scare-mongering in the media and they ought to have more sense. It turned into a real row. They both got huffy and slammed out. We're speaking again, of course, but I guess we lost that argument. It's a dreadful pity because Katie's the one running the risk.

Whoever's right on the vaccination front, Ted and Candy were bound to lose, because they attacked Declan and Emily, effectively calling them stupid, and accusing them of being uncaring parents – no wonder they stormed out. When Ted and Candy were young, doctors all agreed about vaccina-tion – and no one ever argued with doctors anyway. But they need to realise that these days it can be hard for parents to make decisions like this, because expert opinion is often divided – and if the professionals can't agree, how can parents be expected to know what's best? It would have been more productive to put their point of view gently, acknowledging that it's a hard call – because it is. That way, even if they didn't prevail, at least their arguments would have been listened to, rather than rejected out of hand.

When Rene disagrees with her daughter, she prefers to leave well alone, not so much out of principle, but, she says, out of cowardice! 'Bedtimes used to get me going. I'd sit there thinking – that child needs to be in bed – but I never had the courage to say anything!' In fact, Rene wasn't being cowardly – she knows where the parameters lie with her daughter and she decided it wasn't a subject worth risking a row for.

Tackling it Tactfully

How you broach a subject is just as important as when, or whether, you do, but it can be hard to get it right. Sometimes the subject is both immediate and emotive, and if you're not careful, however much you realise the wisdom of keeping quiet, you could end up wading right in without thinking it through. This happened to Vivien.

Our two grandsons Toby and Jake have very different personalities and our daughter-in-law Emma seemed to favour Jake, the younger one. Right from birth he was an 'easier' child, sleeping through the night and so on, whereas Toby was more demanding in many ways. We watched Emma grow into the habit of picking on Toby and comparing him with his little brother: 'Why can't you be more like Jake – *he* doesn't do that . . .' It's true that Toby was naughty, but it seemed to my husband, Richard, and me, that he'd got that way at least partly because of the criticism he was getting. Jake, on the other hand, would watch all this, and very quickly learned what pressed his mum's buttons and how to keep his nose clean, while managing to get his brother into plenty of hot water. We thought Toby didn't feel his mum loved him as much as his brother – even though we knew she did. It upset us because he'd get stressed and miserable. It wasn't doing Jake any good either, learning how to tell tales to such good effect. We talked quietly to our son Hugh a few times, but nothing much changed. Over several years we tried to compensate a bit in emotional terms for all this with Toby, but he didn't know we disagreed with his mum about him; we didn't let him get away with anything and always stuck to Emma's rules.

Then one day I did the unthinkable: I criticised their mum in front of the boys. Jake had just done something naughty, but instead of ticking *him* off, Emma got cross with Toby for not preventing it somehow – as if it was Toby's fault that Jake had misbehaved – and it hadn't been. It seemed to me wrong on so many levels – just one more example of what was going on, and before I could stop myself I said, 'Oh, come on, Emma, you can't say that.' I didn't get angry or say any more, and she did drop it, which took the heat off Toby, but I knew I'd overstepped the mark and put myself in the wrong. We didn't talk about it afterwards but I'm sure Emma thought I was an interfering old bat – and she was right! I was completely out of order and I knew it as I spoke, but it was too late then to take it back. I'd never done anything like that before, or since, and of course if I could go back I'd do it differently. I should have apologised later, too. Emma's a great mum. She loves her kids and she was doing what she thought was right. In theory that should be that, but in practice it sometimes isn't, is it? And you know what? If it made Emma stop and think, even a bit, then I guess it was worth it. My grandchildren are more important than me being top of the popularity poll.

Emma and I talked about it recently, and she says she was quite angry at the time – she thought I was way out of line that day – that she was their mum and it was her call, not mine.

You have to be careful, too, that by talking to one parent and not the other, you don't make them have to take sides. Pointing out what she and Richard felt and why, to both of them *together*, might have created the chance to discuss the whole subject. A chat might have made Emma at least willing to look at it from a different angle, whereas what's seen as a challenge can have the effect of entrenching someone in their view – sides have been drawn up. Whoever was right about the main issue in this instance, the fact you have to face as grandparents is that parents have the final say.

If you find yourself acting impulsively, bite the bullet and apologise. It's the right thing to do and you can use the opportunity to explain why it happened. 'I'm sorry, but I've been worried – this is why . . .' And it can be worth broaching difficult subjects. Ed was worried about his granddaughter being overstretched.

Megan started on the violin when she was four. I thought it was a bit young but her mum and dad were very musical, so I'd always expected them to start her off early. And she seemed to be enjoying it. But by the time she was seven she was having lessons twice a week. Every day when she got in from school they'd start on her to get her fiddle out. She had a whole hour's practice, then there was homework, some- times she'd be going to swimming lessons, dance class, judo – all the stuff that kids do now. She never seemed to have any time to just – you know – be a kid. I thought it was too much – especially the violin. I could see that Megan had lost interest in it. On top of that, she was permanently tired and listless and she caught any bug that was going round at school.

In the end I had a word with her mum and dad. I told them I thought Megan looked under the weather – that

I was worried about her health, and asked them to think about letting her back off the activities a bit – especially the violin. I was a bit afraid of mentioning that because I knew how keen they were on it, but I said what if she gets so fed up she gives up music for good? I suggested they ask Megan what she'd like to do, and they said they'd do that. Sure enough, she wanted to drop the violin. It disappointed them, but Megan perked up straight away. You could see the difference in her. And it worked out for the best, because she really *is* musical – she took up the piano a year later and she's loving that. You can tell, because she doesn't need nagging to practise.

Ed knew that Megan's parents hadn't meant to stretch her so far – they just wanted to give her all the opportunities there were. Seeing things from someone else's point of view made them think again.

If you do decide an issue is important enough to raise, try not to make your children feel they're being judged. You could begin with, 'Have you thought about [whatever the problem is]. This is what's been worrying us – what do you think?'

But if speaking out can be tricky, keeping quiet doesn't necessarily mean you'll win the prize for tact – it all depends on how you do it. Catherine's parents manage to make their views understood without saying anything at all, and still ruffle her feathers in the process. 'Mum and Dad don't actively interfere, but we always know exactly what they think – it just oozes out. We can tell immediately when they disapprove of something.' Catherine hasn't fallen out with her parents, and this shows considerable restraint on her part. After all, how would you feel under a cold shower of silent criticism?

There are other ways we can upset our children, too – like trying to push our rule book on to them. Desiree's mother-in-law, Imogen, tried this.

When my son Lee was born he effectively turned night into day and wouldn't settle well between feeds. Imogen was always telling me how fantastic my partner, Pete, had been as a baby. According to her, he'd gone straight into a four-hour routine from the moment of birth and never cried. He was perfect. She kept on about how I should stick to a timetable. It was my fault, then, that Lee was the way he was!

At first I struggled to do it her way. I'd hassle myself *and* the baby. I'd be for ever calculating how if Lee went down early or late he'd be awake at the wrong time, juggling intervals in my head like a mathematician. It was a night-mare and I drove myself – and Pete – crazy with it. I wanted to be more relaxed about it, so finally I did it my way and eventually it sorted itself out into a routine that worked for us.

Imogen was trying to help by giving what she believed was good advice. It didn't dawn on her that Desiree was taking her comments as criticism, and that they were making things worse. It's probably true, too, that the way she remembered her son's babyhood and how it had really been, had parted company a bit. She was, quite innocently and unintentionally, praising *herself*, and that did nothing to bolster Desiree's confidence. She didn't want to hear how good her mother-in-law had been at something *she* was struggling with – it just made her feel inadequate. It would have been better if Imogen and Desiree had had a conversation that began, 'Have you thought of trying four-hourly feeds? I did it with Pete . . .'

But if you're going to do that, be honest – memory *is* selective – don't just talk about the successes you had, mention the problems too, and what you learned, if anything, from them. Then you're sharing, not trying to dictate.

As grandparents, one of our most important roles is to provide emotional support for our children. Jill thinks her mother, Eleanor, has it right. 'Mum doesn't volunteer an opinion unless she feels very strongly, but when she does she'll ring and say, "I have to just tell you this . . ." I respect her for saying what she thinks – she's been through these things before, and her views are valid. I appreciate her comments. It's funny, there comes a point when you realise you're turning into your parents!'

Probably the best strategy of all is to wait for them to ask. That way you'll know your opinion is wanted.

Facing Facts

There's no doubt that an in-law's role can be tougher than a parent's where grandchildren are concerned. For a start, your son- or daughter-in-law isn't necessarily going to be as receptive to input. That's understandable when you think about it. Your own children might not agree with you about a particular aspect of the way you brought them up, but they'll be able to put it into the context of their whole childhood and take it with a pinch of salt. You don't have that shared background with their partner. Their own experiences and memories are completely different, so they're less likely to give you leeway. Dick found this with his daughter-in-law Kelly.

My son David and his girlfriend have two little girls, Maud

and Lola. They're both under seven, and I think they're very sloppy with them. I told my son he let them get away with murder, and he said, 'Well, Dad, you were really strict with me. I'm not going in for all that severe stuff.' Obviously he told Kelly what I'd said and she got me on my own. She was quite ratty – told me I was out of order even mentioning it. She said I'd given David all sorts of confidence issues he was still struggling with all these years later. I was flabbergasted. David had never said anything to me and I felt a bit betrayed. It was as though I was seeing our whole relationship from another angle – and it wasn't what I'd always thought it was.

I asked David about it over a pint one night and he admitted that he'd once told Kelly about feeling a bit insecure at college. But he said it wasn't a big deal – he didn't feel I'd been a bad dad or anything. It was a real eye-opener.

Kelly obviously wasn't as relaxed as David about his childhood. She felt protective – there's a tigress in most women when it comes to the people they love.

Having a child of your own changes your perspective on a lot of things. David didn't hold a grudge against his father – he knew he'd been loved as a child – but he wanted to avoid creating in his own children feelings he'd experienced himself. This might be hard to take, but it's valid. There are times in life when we come face to face with how others see us, and it can be a salutary experience.

Sometimes what *you* think you're like as a grandparent, and what your children think you're like, can be rather different, too. Andy and Jenny have two boys aged seven and ten. Andy's mother, Joyce, says, 'I *never* interfere – I don't tell them how to bring their children up. That's their job and they're doing it very well.' Jenny, on the other hand, says:

Joyce interferes minutely all the time. She doesn't tell me I'm doing things wrong, or undermine me with the children, but she lives near us and she's involved in everything. She'll phone me and say I should bring two coats for them because it's cold, or remind me not to forget the sun cream, or suggest they should have their eyes tested. I get this constant barrage of demands. But it's *caring*. If they've had a school test she'll ring up to see how they did. She doesn't want their eyes to be bad, and she cares enough to say something about it. She's an amazing person – so well read and a real problem solver. She'll keep on until something's sorted. I was blown away by this amount of interest at first, but I'm used to it now, and I admire it.

Oh, there are aspects of it that drive me potty – she doesn't always treat both boys the same, for example. It looks as though she's favouring one or other, but it's not that at all – she's treating them as individuals with their own needs. And to be honest, there's not a lot to disagree with. She's sweet – she'll say to them, 'Now, do you help your mummy and daddy with that . . . ?' I'd far rather have that level of interest and love than the relative distance we have with my own parents, who love us all, but don't involve themselves in that way. I think I'm lucky.

Joyce is lucky too, that her daughter-in-law feels so relaxed about her involvement. Jenny is clearly completely confident in her role as a parent and doesn't feel threatened by Joyce. A less secure person might not look at it that way. They love and respect each other, and this makes a big difference.

Whatever level of involvement you go in for will depend on the relationship you have with your children, but before you speak up, try to think how you'd have felt if someone had said it to you.

The Question of Abuse

There are some subjects that can be hard to know how to begin to deal with. Abuse is one of them. This is a monstrous word, conjuring up as it does images of horrendous sexual perversion or physical injury. But it isn't always dramatic – it can be a quiet, slow, insidious deprivation of love; the creation of desperate fear and anxiety through excessive shouting and bullying; lack of proper care resulting in cold and hunger. Abuse can come in many forms and be at many levels, and it's sometimes unintentional, not deliberate. How do you tell if it's really happening?

Even if you're seriously worried about an aspect of your grandchild's life you may have pushed it to one side, telling yourself that accusations of this type can break up families irrevocably; that you're imagining things, misinterpreting or over-dramatising a situation – and of course this may be true. But, equally, if something *is* happening, letting it lie out of fear of the consequences is unthinkable. However close you are to your grandchild, it's very likely they won't share this kind of experience with you, because abused children habitually blame *themselves*. So, what to do?

Before you do *anything* else, you need to examine the situation as objectively and cold-bloodedly as possible. Try to think back to any changes in your grandchild, when they began, how long things seem to have been this way.

How you tackle it will then depend on the specific nature of your suspicions. There are organisations you can approach, and leaflets available to give you insights and suggest starting points (see pages 257–8).

The Discipline Factor

You love your grandchildren, but they're not angels, and you might want to put them straight. How do you go about it? Your children's ideas of appropriate behaviour and how to achieve it might mesh completely with your own – but then, again, they might not, so there's room for conflict here. Partly it's to do with the way *we* were brought up.

Our grandparents – and indeed our own parents – had a specific view of the role of children in what was, essentially, an adult world. Children were expected to be courteous, not to interrupt when an adult was speaking, to have good manners, both in general and at the table, to show respect to our elders, consideration for others . . . and those standards probably resonate with our children too. They'll want their own children to be like that – what parent wouldn't? So far, so good.

But in our day it went much further than that – a very long way from the tenderness and solicitude with which we treat our grandchildren now. In our childhood, in just about everything, a child's needs came second to an adult's – especially an elderly adult's. The first pick of the food on the table automatically went to the grown-ups. In fact, it was commonly considered impolite for a child to ask for *anything* at the table – good manners decreed that you had to be offered it. So, when visiting grandparents or other relatives, having eaten the boring obligatory stuff like bread and butter, you might sit there fancying a piece of cake, but knowing that if someone didn't think to offer it, you couldn't have any; and it was rude to ask for second helpings. It sounds incredible now, doesn't it, even to us? Yet it was a normal part of childhood. In any case you were expected to finish all the food on your plate or you didn't get any pudding.

All this, of course, was the aftermath of rationing, and the fact that for years there hadn't been enough food to go round. Waste was a terrible crime. For many of our generation, it still is. The idea is so ingrained that you may still find it difficult to leave food, even when you've had enough. Your children might share those views, but these days it's quite possible that they won't — there's been a revolution in attitudes to food.

Randy's parents, Sylvia and Jonathon, definitely don't agree with him on this subject.

If the kids leave anything on their plates, Dad won't actually tell them directly to eat it up — he'll just come out with a story like, 'My cousin Norris was a fussy eater — if he didn't finish everything, his dad would bring it back at every meal for a week, until he ate it.' Dad thinks he's being funny, he's trying to make a joke, but he means it, too (it's actually a true story). Of course the kids see straight through his ruse, and in any case we don't agree with him. If the children have had enough and leave the rest, we say well done for leaving it, and we don't stop them from having something else. *Everything* our children eat is healthy, so pudding will be fruit or yoghurt anyway. We want them to learn that it's not good to over-eat.

Whether Randy has it right or not, Jonathon is putting himself in the wrong here because his grandchildren feel comfortable ignoring him, knowing their parents are 'on their side'.

If you find yourself completely at odds with your children over something like this, then you only have two options — you can try to persuade them (away from your grandchildren), or leave it alone. If you correct your grandchildren in their own home, in the presence of their parents, knowing they don't agree with you, you're putting your children in a very difficult position: they have to back you up and go against their own established rules, or directly contradict you. Either way sends mixed messages to your grandchildren, who can be quick to see an opening and start to exploit it ('Granddad says I can', 'Mum lets me').

It might undermine your authority with them, too, by convincing them that maybe what you think doesn't count. This is something you absolutely don't want to happen, both for your future credibility in general, and in particular when they're in *your* home, although then there are different ways to handle it (see Chapter 4).

Sometimes discretion can be the better part of valour, as Greta found with her daughter Hilary. 'One day I corrected my granddaughter about something – it wasn't a big deal, but Hilary got cross with me. She said, "It's nothing to do with you, Mum, leave her alone." So now I don't do anything like that – I don't want Hilary to tell me off.' This seems a shame – Hilary is making it clear to her daughter that Grandma has no clout when it comes to discipline, something which might backfire on them all later.

Of course, if you know that you and your children speak with one voice, then you can go ahead without worrying. It's worth having a chat with them about general behaviour expectations and, if there are any differences, coming to some agreement between you about the way to handle things. This can save you all a lot of anxiety, and keep things on an even keel.

Maureen and Robert have three grandchildren under five. They know and agree with their children's views on discipline, but they're still careful. Maureen says, 'If our grand-children misbehave, our way of handling it is to have a word with them, rather than their parents. We just say, quietly, "No, don't do that." It's easier to say it to them, but I tread carefully, and very quickly withdraw if I think I'm going too far. It's a minefield. Our children are sensitive, and I understand that. They're very grown-up – much older than we were when we had *them* – and they know how they want things to be. I don't think we're in a position to interfere.' Robert thinks rather differently. He says, 'I'm old-fashioned. If something's wrong, I feel I need to say it. I don't think you *can* ask too much of children – you have to tell them, and then they'll remember it later in life.' Up to a point Robert's right, but with small children there's a fine line between instilling good basics and seeming impatient. It can be best to go gently.

Roy let his four-year-old grandson, Daniel, get to him, with unfortunate results. 'Daniel was watching me disbudding my show chrysanths. He was obviously interested, and I explained to him that I was taking off the side shoots so the main flower would grow big. He nipped off a main head and I said, "No, we don't do that." I looked up a few minutes later to find him carefully taking off more heads. I was horrified. I said, "DON'T!" in a loud voice and toe-ended him. Of course, I didn't hurt him – just up-ended him with my foot very gently onto the ground. Daniel didn't do it again, but I felt very uncomfortable, and I got into trouble with my son.'

Roy admits now that he shouldn't have done it: it was a knee-jerk reaction because he was concerned for his flowers, rather than a lesson for his grandson – discipline isn't about punishment so much as learning. Roy could have explained that it would spoil the flowers, that they were important to him and that you don't wreck someone's things. If he'd then said, 'Now, if you do that again you'll be in hot water,' he might possibly have been able to claim a tiny sliver of moral high ground. But Roy didn't warn him – and the temptation was too much for a little boy's nature.

Whether Daniel meant to be naughty or had just misunderstood, the punishment wasn't appropriate to the crime. It did teach Daniel a lesson – but of what kind? That grown-ups lash out when something goes wrong; perhaps that his grandfather had a short temper; certainly that he cared about his chrysanthemums, but nothing directly about obedience or respect for other people's possessions.

The Smacking Issue

Over the last fifty years many attitudes have changed, and some of the precepts our parents took for granted have been turned on their heads. Political correctness can drive everyone crazy, whatever their age, but there's no denying that, even allowing for all the weird anomalies, in some ways we live in a more liberal, tolerant and empathetic world. And there's the rub – some people might find it *too* empathetic.

Take corporal punishment – our teachers caned us or hit us with a ruler or slipper. These days teachers can't touch their pupils, let alone hit them. Our parents smacked us routinely and many of us smacked our own children. But now, smacking is definitely frowned on. It's still legal in the UK (just). Under Section 58 of the Children Act, in England and Wales, smacking is legal as long as it doesn't cause swelling, bruises, cuts, scratches or grazes. Scotland has tighter restrictions and in some cases bans it, and Northern Ireland would like to ban it completely. In fact it's likely that smacking will become illegal throughout the UK in the not too distant future (see page 257). It's a very controversial subject – what might have seemed no big deal to you could be anathema to your children. If you smacked them when they were young they're probably not holding it against you, but they're extremely likely to have decided not to do it to their children. And if they don't – you can't.

Max and Barbara's son Will has three daughters aged six, nine and eleven, and in their grandparents' opinion, the nine-year-old is very naughty. Barbara says:

She just runs riot – Will has admitted they can't handle her. They've tried reasoning, explaining, sending her to her room, but nothing has any effect. It just runs off as though she's impervious. She doesn't seem to care. We've wanted to smack her – *ooh* yes, many times – we think it's the only thing that will work, but we don't overstep that mark because Will and his wife, Joanne, don't believe in it. In fact, I spoke to Joanne about it, and asked her what she thought we should all do. She admitted it was a problem. She said, 'I don't know what else to try – she's so different to the other two.' We suggested smacking as a last resort but Joanne won't do it.

Whoever is right here, Max and Barbara are respecting their child's wishes – and that's vital. Smacking could definitely be described as a big issue – this is a subject everyone has deep feelings about. Where you stand is something for you and your children to discuss together rather than handle spontaneously.

Russell and Melanie did this with their daughter Rhoda who says, 'We do smack our daughters, very occasionally, when we think nothing else will do, and we're quite happy for our parents to do the same. We've talked about it and we all agree on the way to do it. We tell them why what they're doing is naughty, warn them about what will happen if they do it again, and then use the slap as the last resort. We trust Mum and Dad completely, and it's very important for us all to discipline them the same way.'

There was a movement in the early 1970s, which came

loosely under the hippie umbrella, and called itself free expression. Under this very trendy (anti)regime, as a means of developing their personality, children were encouraged to express themselves in any way that seemed appropriate to them without adult reprimand of any kind. So smashing milk bottles on the doorstep, say, would be regarded as 'experimenting' rather than naughtiness. Discipline-free schools were set up to train children of all ages – right through their teens – in the mindset that they should discipline themselves, and that basically any kind of behaviour was OK in the path to self-discovery. Some people thought this made sense – that it would teach children self-control rather than having rules forced upon them; others believed that given human nature, it was wacky and unrealistic, and still others were convinced it was anarchistic and actively dangerous.

Free expression was regarded by some experts as the cutting-edge of educational thinking and so, though it was never widely embraced in its pure form, aspects percolated through society. It had an effect on a whole generation of teaching and child-rearing practices. In fact, it could well have helped to give birth to some of the methods – sound *and* dodgy – used today. Whether you were a born-again believer in free expression, a member of the caning brigade, or somewhere in the middle, you would have been keenly aware of the arguments, and the chances are that you felt strongly about it and argued vehemently for your point of view with your peers and your own parents. It was a political hot potato.

Theories come and theories go but, if you're tempted now to discount your children's views on discipline, whatever they are, it's worth remembering how you felt about free expression at the time. You didn't like anyone telling *you* what to think, did you?

These days the media has enormous influence on parenting styles – TV has popularised the concept of 'the naughty step', which is more or less the third-millennium equivalent of standing a child in a corner. (True to modern marketing principles, it's now possible to buy a branded naughty step to sit your child on.)

It all goes to show that, while interpretations vary, some ideas (good and bad) never go away. But before you point that out to your children, try to remember that each generation has to determine its own standards, and while you might have encountered something before, to them it will feel new, and they have to evaluate its usefulness for themselves. And there *are* subtle differences. Being made to stand in a corner was primarily a punishment – you were in disgrace and everyone could see this. The naughty step – or time out, or any of the modern equivalents – involves a chat with the child about what they did wrong and why, and they're supposed to use the time to think about what they did, and then apologise, before they come back into the fold. In other words, it's meant to be constructive.

Magical Methods

The wonderful thing about being a grandparent is that, in our grandchildren's eyes at least, we're very special people – we can work magic. In practical terms this means there are plenty of ways for us to keep them on the straight and narrow without resorting to blows – or even telling them off – especially when they're small. And this gives us some advantages over their parents.

Parents represent routine – bread and butter, meat and potatoes. They're for homework-chasing, making you tidy your bedroom, telling you what to do – that's their job. Whereas *us*, well, we're completely for fun. Naturally they have fun with their parents, but not all the time. When we're with them, life's a beach.

The fact that they associate us purely with enjoyment means that when we're around they're in a different frame of mind, they're up for it – whatever it is. We might be doing routine things, like the school run, for example (see Chapter 5), but even if that's the case, and even if we do it every day, it's still special because in their world we're celebrities, and they know that with us they're going to get almost unlimited attention. They don't have to misbehave or act up to achieve it, because it's there on a plate. The nature of the relation-ship between grandparents and grandchildren is unique in this respect.

Children need their parents to give them boatloads of love, but not necessarily all of their time. The most devoted parent in the world, whether working or not, can't – and probably shouldn't – devote every single waking second to his/her offspring. Children need to feel completely secure, but they also have to realise the whole world doesn't revolve round them, and that their parents have other responsibilities in their lives, too.

But you're different. From your grandchildren's point of view, you're on their team, at their disposal; you go to visit *them*, so you're less likely to be waving them away while you load the dishwasher, unload the tumble-dryer or argue with the plumber on the phone. These things might happen when they visit you, but even then it isn't the same as at home (see Chapter 4). So with grandparents, they're predisposed to be cheerful and cooperative, which means that when they do start to act up, as all children will, we can employ our charms to wangle them out of it.

Joy developed a trick with her granddaughters, aged two and four.

I was staying with my son's family and trying to get the two girls off to school and nursery. They were stringing it out, ignoring me, squabbling with each other and refusing to fetch their shoes – you know the kind of thing. I could have raised my voice, but they were already taking no notice, so what would have been the point? I just said, 'OK, upstairs for shoes. How do you want to climb the steps – as a giraffe or a lion?' I showed them how to walk like a giraffe, stretching their necks and pretending to duck their heads for the ceiling, and how to growl like a lion. They giggled their way upstairs as one of each, and forgot about bickering. We do it often now for that and other boring chores like going to the loo. They suggest different animals, dinosaurs, ballerinas, space ships, motor bikes – there's no limit really. They love it and remind me if I forget.

Young children are very suggestible – they have a vivid imagination that's wide open to stimulation, so Joy's got a double whammy here – she's distracting them *and* making them think about what it's like to be something or someone else. Myrna and Steven have another way with their grandchildren James and Lucy. Steven says, 'They're five and seven and if they start bickering, we just copy them, putting our hands on our hips and echoing them in silly voices – it always works because we sound so daft – they just crack up.' This could have another advantage: it might make James and Lucy think about what they sound like when *they're* squabbling, and discourage them from doing it (you can always hope).

It's easy to distract very young children, and older ones can be deflected from whatever strop they're throwing too. You can just say, 'Look, I'm going to pop to the shop for a loaf of bread – shall we go and see what they've got for tea?' Or, 'How about coming upstairs with me to find that book

Granddad mislaid?' Or, maybe, 'Who feels like a walk to the park/giving me a hand with the supermarket shopping?' In fact you can use anything that's appropriate to their age and interests, as long as it doesn't feel like a bribe; and as long as you don't seem to be siding with them against their parents.

Spoiling Them

Given that our grandchildren are expecting wall-to-wall one-to-oneness, it can be hard to draw the line between fulfilling their (and our) wish for this and spoiling them. We want to please them – we want them to be happy; to enjoy us to the full.

A major difference between our own childhood and our grandchildren's is the way they can bask in the sunshine of our approval. When we were small, we had to be on our best behaviour round adults. 'Children should be seen and not heard' was the mantra. Our own childhood might have been happy, but how incredibly restricted and controlled that world seems now, compared with the riotous carnival enjoyed by our grandchildren just two generations later. They can be completely relaxed and natural with us, content and secure in our love and full of love for us in return. Far from waiting to be offered what's on the table – or anywhere else for that matter – they feel perfectly comfortable in asking for what they want. *We* might have had to do without second help-ings, but our grandchildren are under no such constraints with us. And surely that's a better way? As long as they ask politely and don't just expect to get everything their heart desires . . . and we don't give it to them.

The key to fixing the line between simply pleasing them and gratifying their every whim lies in knowing what their expectations are. It's lovely to give them treats, but that isn't the same as spoiling them all the time. We need to help them learn the meaning of the word 'no'.

Jared says his mother, Ina, spoils his children completely. 'Mum lets them do anything they want; they get away with murder. I try to tell her it's wrong, but she doesn't listen, she just says they're her grandchildren and that's what she's there for. So the kids play us off against each other. It's giving them all the wrong ideas. Of course grandmas are meant to spoil them, but there have to be limits or your kids will just run rings round you.' What Ina doesn't appreciate is that her grandchildren have learned how to take advantage of the differences between her rules – or rather lack of them – and their parents' rules. She might be fine with it now, but it will come back to bite her later, because they're learning from her how to be manipulative, and maybe selfish. And that's not fair on *them*.

Pam and Dean have similar problems with Dean's mother, Audrey, who can't say no to her granddaughters. Dean says, 'Mum's really soft with the girls. They get anything they want – sweets, cake – you name it. Pam tells her we don't give them chocolate just before bedtime, but Mum does it anyway.' This puts Pam in a very difficult position, especially when they're at her mother-in-law's house. She says:

> Audrey quite often gives them sweets just before they're due to have a meal, and of course they're hungry, so they eat them. I'm sitting there thinking – they'd be much better off with some proper food – should I ask if I can cook for them? It's not my kitchen and not my mum so I'm embarrassed to say anything. I get on OK with her and I don't want to spoil it. My own mum and dad are just the opposite. Once when we went to stay with them, they got on at me

for not giving the children enough greens. Mum told the kids to eat everything up and it really shocked them – they cried their eyes out. Mum wasn't cross, but they thought they were being told off. Their other granny had never said anything like that.

Pam's mum wasn't being tough on them at all, but she was applying rules they weren't familiar with from a grandparent, and this threw them. Whether your inclination is to be firm or to let them do their own thing, it can be confusing for children if it's at odds with what their parents do. It's important to be consistent, and can be worth sacrificing some of the letter of your own laws (in either direction) to achieve that. So, if your children's parameters aren't exactly the same as yours, try to create a united front.

However you feel about discipline, you want to do your best for your grandchildren, and that means working with their parents, rather than against them. This might sound obvious, but it's easy to get tied up in the issues and lose sight of the main event – the children themselves. Experts say children are most comfortable when they're given recognisable limits, but it's not just *what* you apply that needs to be consistent, but *how* you apply it. Jeremy and Philippa have three-year-old twin girls. Philippa doesn't agree with the way her mother, Janet, disciplines them.

Mum and I have the same rules, but she doesn't always stick to them – it seems to depend on the mood she's in, or how busy she is. One minute they can be doing something they're not supposed to and she'll just ignore it, then the next time they do it she's down on them like a ton of bricks. They don't know where they stand. The end result is that they're quite naughty because they try it on – they're testing her to see what she does. Kids do skate close to the line! Then when I step in they throw a fit, and I can't always depend on her to back me up. I'm working myself up to have a word with my mother about it before it becomes a real problem. I think we need to sort it out before they get into that twelve-year-old pubescent thing – I can see it coming and they're only three!

Phillippa's right to talk to her mother, but she needs to tackle this gently. Opening with something like, 'You know, you let the girls get away with murder' will just put Janet on the defensive. Instead, she needs to wait until they've been naughty and say, 'The last time they did that you let them get away with it/you were cross with them – what's your thinking? Was there a reason?' That will start a discussion.

There's often a difference, between the way a grandma and a granddad operate. Des and Beatrice have seven grand-children, and although they're completely consistent as far as basic rules are concerned, they each deal with them in slightly different ways. Des says:

I don't spoil my grandchildren – although I suppose I'd support them in anything legal. I don't know what you'd call that! In general, though, I demand certain standards from them – their parents think I'm critical, too hard on them, and maybe I do say more than I should, but I'm a priest and in my job I see a lot of people who've destroyed themselves, who never reach their potential. I don't want that to happen to *them*. The kids know exactly where they are with me and I don't think they appreciate me less for it. I tend to tease them a lot, wind them up, but I get my message over and they know what I'm up to, even if their parents don't always realise it. Our influence can never be the same as theirs, but it's very powerful, and we should use it to support them.

Des is very clear on where the boundaries lie for him. Beatrice says, 'I think I'm more of an anxious grandma – I worry about them. I don't fuss, but my concern is for their day-to-day happiness and comfort. I'm very aware that grand-children come almost without responsibility, because they're not *ours*, and so we have to be very careful of what we do and how we do it.' Des adds, 'Beatrice spoils them just a bit and I have to apply the brakes. She's soft with them – in other words, she's perfect!'

What kind of a grandparent are you? It's worth taking an objective look at yourself – and not baulking at what you see. After all, everything you do, you do in love.

BEFORE YOU INTERFERE

Stop and Think

Is the issue important enough to risk a row?

Could it have long-term effects on the child?

Might it have long-term consequences?

Is it just a knee-jerk reaction?

How are your children likely to react?

What's the best way to tackle it?

IF YOU SPEAK UP

Don't

Make accusations or judge your children.

Lose your temper.

Try to boss them about.

Lecture them.

Speak out in front of your grandchildren.

Criticise your children in front of your grandchildren.

Do

Remember – these are their children, not yours.

Have a private chat.

Approach the subject calmly.

Listen to your children's views.

Be prepared to admit you're wrong.

Keep a sense of humour.

AVOIDING DISCIPLINE DANGERS

Agree strategies and rules with your children and stick to
  them – be a team.

Agree on acceptable standards of behaviour for your
  grandchildren – and you.

Be consistent – with yourself and with their parents.

Avoid siding with them against their parents.

Explain to children why what they're doing is wrong.

Try to distract them rather than getting cross.

Remember that discipline isn't about punishment – it's about
  learning.

Avoid making yourself popular at the expense of your
  children.

4

The Grandchild Invasion

Having children is a rite of passage into the adult world; you've gone through a door marked 'grown-ups'. But when your grandchildren are born, a door closes – the one into old age – and you stay on this side of it. You don't pass through because your grandchildren hold you back. They keep you young. Through them you can revisit your own childhood and youth. And that's not just because you're telling them stories about your past. It goes much deeper. Your grandchildren enable you to remember all the joys, insecurities, triumphs and anxieties you experienced so intensely as a child, and then lost among the clutter of the years. You live them again through their eyes, and rediscover what it's like to *feel* young. At the same time, the memories of your days as a young parent become more vivid (and perhaps more accurate) as the present pageant unfolds in living colour. It's like going back in time.

Grandchildren can keep you in the young world longer in a physical sense too. Because they arrive about the time you're retiring, or thinking of moving and/or downsizing, their appearance can change your thinking about appropriate living space and location – dramatically.

A lot has been written about the special bond between the older generation and the young, and there are plenty of complex theories about why it happens. But at bottom it's simple – there's no barrier to understanding and love. There's no agenda, no competition. The experience of age and the openness of youth together create a situation where complete trust and confidence can exist. Your grandchildren get – and absolutely know they'll get – nothing less than total love and support from you and, in turn, you know they accept you without question for who you are, and love you right back. It's more than special – it's marvellous.

Being together, spending time with your grandchildren, is an enormous, endless jackpot that just keeps pouring out at your feet. For them, you're a bottomless well of empathy. What's more, you belong to them – you're *theirs*, and they're constantly marking their territory.

Having your family to visit is good fun for everyone, but capturing the children without their parents is especially wonderful, because you make a different kind of connection – you're not just in loco parentis on a practical level, you're an extension of their parents emotionally, and it can bring you closer, even when they're small babies. Their parents get a good deal, too – days off from the joys of child-rearing, time to remember they're still people, not just somebody's mum and dad, periods for pleasure, or just the chance to do major chores like decorating.

It's an upheaval, it's tiring, and you might end up with orange juice on your Axminster, but it's worth it. Wherever you live in relation to them, and however rarely or often you see them, you have a profound effect on each other – and it's all good. The more you can get together, the more you all benefit. You've got the elixir of youth on tap, and they've got the good fairy and the wizard Merlin on permanent speed dial – who can lose?

Making It Happen

Having your grandchildren to visit at any time is a good thing to do, but it's even better if you can make it happen regularly enough for everyone to take it for granted. That way they'll be relaxed with you, you'll be comfortable with what a visit involves, and their parents won't be breathing down your neck with anxiety – either about their children or you.

How to Suggest It

It can be a good idea to start when your grandchildren are babies. All parents need a break sometimes. They'll be feeling the strain, but they'll worry no one can care for their baby like they can and that it's somehow wrong of them to hand it over and take a break – or even to want to. So it's worth suggesting you take over, maybe for just a few hours – even an afternoon off can feel like a long weekend when you're tired and up to your ears in baby. Burt and Nell look after their grandson when their daughter-in-law Jacqueline goes swimming. 'Jacqueline just drops Aaron off with a couple of bottles and goes to the pool. It's all very casual – no big deal.' Making a habit out of it in this way can gradually lead to longer visits. Another way to introduce the idea would be to stay over with *them*. Cora and Miles did this when their daughter Jessie's baby Athene was a few months old.

> I used to stay overnight and babysit when Jessie and her partner, Griff, wanted to be out really late. Because they didn't have a spare room, I slept with Athene. Jessie would express milk, put it in the fridge, and I'd do the middle of the night and early morning feeds so she and Griff could get some shut-eye. It was fantastic. Athene would wake up crying, and I'd go over to her cot, pick her up and she'd give me this wonderful beaming grin, as if I was the most important person in the world to her – which I suppose I was at that moment! She'd lie there smiling away while I changed her nappy. Then we'd settle down and I'd give her a bottle. It felt like being a new mum again myself. All the love I had for my daughter as a baby seemed to flow back and into Athene, and I'd look down and notice the similarities between them – the little gestures Jessie had made that I'd forgotten. I got to experience all over again those moments only parents enjoy: that special closeness you feel with your baby in the middle of the night.
>
> I suggested to Jessie that her dad and I could have Athene for a weekend while they went off somewhere to relax, and they jumped at it. After all, they knew she'd be fine. They left her with enough equipment to sink a battleship and we had a great time looking after her. It was a revelation. We knew what to do, of course, and fell into our old routine

without even discussing it. The whole thing was a breeze – when she woke in the night, Miles would go off to warm the milk and make us a cup of tea while I changed her nappy, and then we fed her, just as we'd done with our own two. It seemed to wind the clock right back – we were twenty-two again. But it was much more fun the second time around without all the little worries and niggles you get when you're new parents.

Athene's nine now and sees us as an extension of her mum and dad. We did the same with her sisters and we regularly have them all to stay. It's home from home for them.

The familiarity Cora established right from the start with her first granddaughter was a terrific bonus – not just for her, but because it led to a close relationship for all of them. It worked for Cora, because she and her daughter were both sure she could cope. That wasn't quite the case for Lillian. 'When my son and his wife had their first baby, I waited for them to ask me to have him overnight but they didn't, so I didn't push myself forward. I think now that perhaps I wasn't that confident. Maybe if I'd had more than one child myself I'd have felt more expert. Anyway, it hasn't made any difference in the long run. I've got three grandsons now and they come to stay all the time.' If your children don't offer, bear in mind that what Lillian says is true – you'll still have plenty of time as they get older. But don't be afraid to mention it; they might be hanging back because they think *you* don't want to do it.

Glynis didn't feel she saw her two grandsons often enough.

It's true we were all busy, but time slips by and I'd look up and realise that three or four months had gone by without me seeing the boys. They were five and two, and changing all the time. I didn't want to miss it, so I asked them all down for the weekend and over a glass of wine, when the children were in bed, I told my son and his wife what I felt. I said I hadn't wanted to intrude on their lives but I felt really distanced from them. And I said how lovely it would be for me to take the children while they went off for a dirty weekend somewhere, for example. They were amazed; they said it hadn't occurred to them. They just hadn't realised I'd be up for it. They were trying to give *me* space! Things are much better now.

Of course there could be other reasons for them not asking you. Shelley hasn't seen much of her new grandson so far. 'My son Keith and his girlfriend live a fair drive away. They have a lot of friends of their own age who have babies, and I suppose they want to spend time with them. It's natural – they have a lot going on in their lives. And we're busy too. We still have two teenage kids at home and we're both working full-time, so we haven't pushed it.' Still, it's a pity Shelley isn't getting the opportunity to take her grandson even for a short while. But some families don't work in this way. It doesn't mean they're not close.

Lester and Morag didn't have their grandson Rhys to stay at all to begin with. Morag says, 'They never asked us, but it was right for them. It's what they felt comfortable with. We didn't mind. In fact, I wouldn't have liked them to leave him with us in the first year anyway, I think *I* wouldn't have been happy about it, if I'd been them. We were there as a back-up. It was fine by us.' For your children, just to know you're there can be a terrific relief – even if they never need to call on you.

The arrival of a second or third baby can be a good opportunity to start inviting the older sibling(s) to stay. You could suggest to your children they might like a break, so they can concentrate some TLC on the youngest – something that can be hard to provide with other children in the house. Basil and Dora did this with their two granddaughters, Roxana and Serena.

When our grandson Travis was starting to walk, we offered to have his sisters, who were four and two, for a weekend. We put it to them that they could concentrate on Travis in a way they hadn't been able to before, for fear of making the girls jealous. Our son and his wife loved it because they'd been feeling a bit guilty about that, and the girls were pleased as Punch because this was for them – it seemed a very grown-up thing to do. It started something, and while we do have all three of them now, the girls ask to come on their own, too. It's great, because we can take them to places and do things that their brother's too young for.

Basil and Dora are keen to spend time with their grandchildren. But not all grandparents want to get so deeply involved. Nerys's parents, Keith and Shelley, like to keep a level of independence.

Mum and Dad adore the children, but they haven't looked after them on their own. They've offered, but I don't really think they want to, and we haven't taken them up on it. We all love each other, but we're not close emotionally: I'm not with my mum and she wasn't with hers. We don't discuss feelings. But they look forward to coming to stay with us for things like Christmas, and the kids get excited about that. I understand how they feel. They worked very hard all their lives, then retired early and bought a smaller house. They're not well off, but they wanted to enjoy the fruits of their labour – go on holidays, things like that. It's very important to them, something they've looked forward to for a long time, so they're careful to guard their freedom. And Dad's got cancer, so they want to live life now, while they can. My husband's parents are just the opposite – they have the children all the time. Mum and Dad think they're off their rockers. They say, 'Don't they *want* a life?'

It all depends how you define *life*. Keith and Shelley want to use their retirement to be completely free of ties and responsibilities – why not? Especially since there's the possibility that Keith's health will deteriorate. There's no 'best' way to be a grandparent, and you don't need to feel guilty about your choices – just work out what feels right to you.

Fitting Them Into Your Life

Having your grandchildren for the occasional afternoon or overnight might be enough, or you might want to be more hands-on. Lewis and Corinne see a lot of their six grandchildren. Corinne says, 'We often have them to stay without their parents, who all work and are quite happy to hand them over for a weekend. Of course we love to have our children too, but it's special when the grandchildren are on their own. We don't often get all six of them together, but one set or other is here for a week at half term or in the summer holidays. In fact, I think they'd let us take them for much longer if we volunteered, and the only reason we don't is that *we* have stuff to do as well! It always hurts me when I have to say no, but sometimes we have to be strong – those kids are like a drug.'

When you have a relaxed relationship with your children, it's easy to accommodate each other, and be honest about saying yes or no. If you're not on such close terms it can be harder. Whether you feel deprived, or think you're being taken advantage of, have a quiet word. Say how much you love them all, but explain how you feel and why, without getting heated.

Keeping Up the Pace

After years of having your house to yourself, the presence of young children, even for an afternoon, can feel like an invasion from outer space – alien creatures with a different lifestyle, strange needs and unusual appetites – exotic and interesting, but a challenge.

Clifford often has his three granddaughters to stay. 'The girls range in age from eighteen months up to six, and one Sunday teatime, just after they'd left, I caught sight of myself in the hall mirror. My hair was stuck up, I hadn't shaved all weekend, and I had bags under my eyes because I'd been awake in the night when one of them threw up. I was wearing ancient sweat pants and a scruffy T-shirt – I looked a wreck! But it's definitely all worth it!' Clifford is revelling in his grandchildren, but he does subscribe to the old chestnut about being able to 'hand them back'. As he says, 'It's lovely when they come – and it's lovely when they go!'

One way to keep up with the pace is to try and take a short nap every day. Very young children usually have a sleep themselves after lunch, so instead of using the time for something like tidying up, get your head down. Kevin and Vera's grandchildren had got beyond the afternoon sleep stage, so instead they suggested a quiet time. 'They loved the Richard Scarry books, so we said they could have a "Richard Scarry moment", and go to lie down (in separate bedrooms) with one of his books each to look through. They nearly always dozed off. Now they're older they choose whatever books they want and even if they don't actually go to sleep, they're quiet for about half an hour which means *we* can get forty winks!' Kevin and Vera are taking what the army call 'combat naps' – it's acknowledged that even short sleeps in the middle of a busy schedule can make a huge difference to your energy levels.

Learn to take opportunities as they arise and to take things in your stride. Having, for perhaps the first time in your life, gained control of the contents of your cupboards, you'll need to relinquish this luxury for a whole new set of bulky paraphernalia. For the second time round you'll have cots, high chairs, booster seats, bottle warmers, bottles, infant cutlery, bricks, cuddly toys, books, dolls, toy trains. Your garage and shed will once again be a labyrinth of bicycles, scooters, miniature wheelbarrows . . . But rushing round trying to keep things tidy is a waste of your precious energy – it's truly amazing how much mess just one child can make. Gloria, a grandmother of three, doesn't bother. 'I learned when they were babies that grandchildren don't travel light, and even an infant who can't move under its own steam will effectively trash your house from the second it's carried through the door. As they grow, this just gets worse, so I'm cool about it. Instead of trailing round picking up after them, I resign myself to chaos and just enjoy being with them. Cushion-plumping and fussing with the vacuum cleaner would only take me away from things I could be doing with them, and making them tidy up constantly would bore them rigid. The time I spend with them is too precious for all that. I have a purge when they've gone.'

But should you clear the decks – move your favourite vase and any other breakable objects? Or do you grit your teeth and teach them not to touch? Barty and Deirdre decided on the latter approach with their two-year-old grandson, Kane.

Deirdre says, 'We had a porcelain kingfisher on a corner table. It was lovely – very colourful and lifelike, and Kane was fascinated by it. He's an inquisitive child and he climbed up and got hold of it. Of course he broke it and then screamed blue murder. He knew he shouldn't have done it and was really upset and sorry. I told him off very gently, and explained why he shouldn't touch Nana's things. Next time he came he brought me a picture of a kingfisher he'd drawn, bless him. I deliberately didn't move my ornaments because they have to learn, don't they? I thought it was better to teach him to understand when I said *no*.' How you tackle this one will depend on the age and temperament of your grandchildren, the value and fragility of your knick-knacks – and on your own nerves!

Coping With the Details

There's more to the grandchild invasion than toys all over the floor. These days, the high incidence of allergies and conditions like asthma and eczema, plus ever-changing advice on diet, can mean you have to adopt a whole new way of thinking while they're in residence. Allergies, and preventing them, can be a particular difficulty. It's considered universally sensible to omit salt and nuts from every baby's diet for the first twelve months, but there are many other foods that, while not actually prohibited, are discouraged (see page 259). And it's not just food, as Charles has found.

My six granddaughters are *all* allergic to various soaps, shampoos, creams, suntan lotions and what have you. One set has eczema and can't have any soap in the bath at all, or shampoo. They have to be washed in plain water. Then they need to be creamed all over every night before bed. That's fine – it's easy to remember. The other set don't have eczema, but they do react badly to various brands – and they're all different! I'll pick up a bottle that says children's suntan cream on it and someone will say, 'No, Granddad, that's not mine!' We keep a stock of the correct brands and I don't want to make any of them itch, of course, so I'm careful. But I do sometimes have a senior moment and slosh something into the bathwater that shouldn't be there.

Maybe the best thing is to write a list and keep it where you keep the products – then you can check it each time they come. The same applies to risky foods – a list behind a kitchen cupboard door should keep things simple.

Making a Meal of It

Meals can be a problem when your grandchildren come to stay without their parents. You'll probably escape the worst of any food battles that are going on between them, simply because you're *not* their parents, but there are plenty of opportunities for strife. If they're picky eaters at home, they're likely to be picky with you, and if you don't want *your* mealtimes to turn into battlegrounds, you need a strategy. One way is just to relax, and not try to reform them; on the other hand, you're in a good position to influence them subtly.

There's no point giving them a whole meal of unfamiliar food and expecting them to polish it off. True, some children are cosmopolitan and sophisticated in their tastes, and welcome new gastronomic experiences with enthusiasm, but many won't – it all depends on how and what they eat at home. If your grandchildren are budding gourmets, that's great. If they're not, try introducing one new, or previously unfavoured food alongside things you know they like. If it looks interesting, they might be tempted to try it. Rose did this with her granddaughters, aged three and four.

I'd cooked chops and they were having green beans, which I know are their favourite, but I put a few Brussels sprouts on the table too. The girls are fairly adventurous, but they looked at them and said, 'What are them green things, Grandma?' I told them, and they said, a bit dubiously, that they'd have a go. I ended up having to cook some more – they ate the whole bowlful! In our family, sprouts are always 'them green things' now. The same happened when I made chicken soup. I didn't expect them to be very enamoured – soup can be a challenge for young children, because it's full of strange bits. But I added some squash, and put it in the blender so it was smooth and a lovely colour. I called it 'golden soup' and they polished it off. These days, they ask for it.

In fact, they sometimes ring me up before they come to stay and request things: 'Can we have Yorkshire puddings, Gran?' And the five-year-old has said, eating pastry, 'I *love* ends of pie.' I'm thrilled to bits, because it means they trust me, and if I do introduce something they haven't had before, they'll have a go.

It's not that what you're offering is any better than what they get at home; it's just that, once again, the magic dust of grandparenthood wafts over a potential problem. It helps, too, if you personalise food, especially if they can do it themselves – like putting their initials onto the pastry lids of individual pies, or marking the top of their own little shepherd's pie. Allowing them to serve themselves from dishes on the table is more appealing than handing out portions because it's a grown-up thing to do – and after all, no one can know exactly how much they want of any particular thing, can they? It's hardly fair to serve them with an amount *you* think they ought to eat and then beat them up for not finishing it. If they're allowed to serve themselves, you can encourage them to have modest helpings, so they can always go back for more.

It's worth remembering that there are some things that almost universally, young children don't fancy — fruit cake, cream and salad, for example. But while they might turn up their noses at lettuce, or grated carrots in French dressing, they'll happily crunch their way through a whole raw carrot, runner bean, or tomato, so give 'em those instead. Children are individuals, and they'll have their own likes and dislikes, just as grown-ups do. You'll be able to tell, because fads will come and go but the genuine hates will stick around.

Potatoes seem to appeal to all children, in some form or another, and not just chips — although it's true that crispy *anything* equals good. With that in mind, slide your healthy mashed potato into the oven or under the grill until it's brown and tasty, and don't have roast potatoes just for Sunday lunch — cooked in olive oil until they're crusty, they'll be devoured with any meal. Jacket potatoes can be off-putting, but if you cut them in half, scoop out the middle and mash it with grated cheese, bits of ham or crispy bacon, put it back in the skins and slap them under the grill to brown — result! They might not eat the skin, but you can't have everything. As with adults, presentation is important. Instead of giving them a whole, single piece of fruit they might get bored with, make up a tempting plate of sliced apples, pears, orange segments, grapes, strawberries — whatever's in season — and present it at mid-morning, then sit back and watch it disappear.

Again, just like adults, children are susceptible to atmosphere, as Leslie and Alvin have found with their three small granddaughters. 'At least once during a stay, they want a "dinner party". Basically this means we dim the kitchen lights and have cloth napkins and candles on the table. Alvin and I eat with them, and they try very hard to be polite. They love it and I'm sure it helps with their table manners.' What Leslie is doing is making food fun – an adventure, not a chore.

Babies are a much easier proposition. Bonnie has three grandchildren ranging from three to twelve months.

As soon as they came off the bottle I made up what I call 'power cubes' to keep in the freezer. They're steamed and pureed vegetables and fruit, like apple, sweet potato, courgette, spinach, squash, carrot – you name it. I cooked batches of meat stock, without salt, and, when they were a little bit older, casseroles, packed with things that are good for them. I froze them in ice-cube trays and stored the cubes in plastic bags. They're easy to defrost and saved the kids dragging jars with them, or faffing about with a food mill and a yelling baby. It didn't take long, because I did it between their visits, when I was cooking something similar. Another bonus is that they're very highly flavoured, so the children got used to all sorts of different tastes from a very early age.

Keeping Them in Line

It's important to keep up continuity when grandchildren come to stay with you. If they're going through the process of potty training, for example, you'll need to carry on with whatever system their parents have set in motion. This is for two reasons: one, you don't want to set them back; two, if for some reason they *do* fail to progress, you don't want to get the blame . . . If your children are devotees of the 'once an hour, every hour' school of thought, you'll simply need to bite the bullet and get on with it. Your grandchildren will find it tedious, but you have to be strong. Young children invest very high emotional stakes in the process of becoming dry, but they're only little, and they'll forget, so they depend on you to keep them up to it. They'll be very upset if you fail them and they wet themselves. Of course, they will, inevitably, have an accident at some point.

Delia's granddaughter Amber is nine. 'Amber was staying with us when she was about eighteen months old, and going through the sitting on the potty period. She'd just been on it for about twenty minutes without results, and was playing in the bedroom, naked, while I popped across the landing to fetch her pyjamas. I came back to find she'd pulled out the bottom dresser drawer. She was standing in it, looking down – she'd poohed in it, of course. She started to cry, but I cuddled her and told I wasn't cross. How could I be? It was messy – but very funny.' Hanging on to your sense of humour is vital – it makes things easier for both you and the children.

If you and your children have an agreed method of discipline and the same behaviour expectations (see Chapter 3), then keeping them in line minus parents should be straightforward, but if you don't completely mesh, then problems could lurk.

Sanjiv says his mum makes up her own rules. 'Actually, Mum doesn't *have* any rules. When our son Raj goes to visit her, she and her sisters just let him run riot. He gets anything he wants, eats all kinds of rubbish, and never gets corrected for anything. I'd be worried that it would damage Raj, but he doesn't see her all that often, and seems to understand that when he gets home ordinary conditions apply, so he gets back to normal within a day or so.' Two things are happening here: Sanjiv's mother probably feels inclined to spoil her grandson because she doesn't see very much of him, but she might get to see him more often if she didn't spoil him so much.

Sometimes you *can* get away with differences, as Fanny and Godfrey found. 'We had our grandson Dean to stay with us for a few days while our daughter-in-law Caitlin recovered from flu. She's not very strict about things like eating up, but while he was with us, Godfrey always quietly insisted that he did. One day Caitlin arrived in time for breakfast, and with his mum at the table, Dean left his toast – he knew she wouldn't make him eat it. But just then Godfrey walked into the room and just *looked* at Dean. Without a word, he picked his toast up and finished it. Caitlin never even knew what had happened.' Almost certainly Dean reverted to his normal behaviour as soon as he got home. You might make a permanent and dramatic difference to your grandchildren's behaviour, but then again, you probably won't and, with this in mind, you have to decide where you're going to draw the line when they're with you. It's reasonable to expect a certain standard of politeness and obedience, but it's probably safer and kinder not to scare them with a lot of unfamiliar do's and don'ts.

It's likely anyway, that their level of naughtiness will be much less than when they're at home, but if they do misbehave, whatever form of reprimand you give, try to leave it at that. In other words, don't tell their parents. After all, once they've been brought to book by you, why should they have to go through it all again? And if their parents find out, that's very likely to happen – there will be an inquest, either in front of you, or later – 'Why did you do that at Grandma's?' Another telling off, even a very mild one, hardly seems fair, does it?

Of course, that won't necessarily stop them from doing it

to *you*, if you break one of their parents' rules. They won't be sneaking on you, just talking honestly about their stay. And children have minds of their own, so things they overhear, they're likely to repeat. Be warned . . .

Reaping the Benefits

The joys of having your grandchildren around you are hard to exaggerate. There's such a lot you can learn from each other, so much pleasure to get and give. Yes, they'll wear you out; by the time they leave you'll be frazzled, surveying the wreckage of your home, or at least its total disruption, with dismay. But, by golly, it's worth every scattered crumb and frozen pea on your kitchen floor, every sticky fingerprint on your French windows. You'll forget the muddy footprints and dead leaves up your stairs as you gaze sentimentally at the row of small wellington boots by the back door. There isn't anything – really there isn't – to beat the total fun of becoming a child again along with them.

And it does *them* good. Lorraine, who has two grandchildren, aged eleven and eight, likes to make a contrast between their ordinary lives and the time they spend with her. 'These days children do so much – they have a fuller day than a politician. There's only one afternoon in the week when my grandchildren are free to come round after school and I make a point of letting them relax and slow down after their busy day. We don't have a schedule, I don't rush them – it's just a piece of time for them to do their own thing. Quite often they just want to sit quietly and draw – that tells me something. They come to me for their own space. Everything in children's lives seems to be programmed – too controlled, like those meaningless electronic games.'

Lorraine has a point. It can be tempting, when your grandchildren come to you, to plan an exciting programme of events and visits, and while these are enormous fun for you all, there's no need to break your back – or the bank – filling up every single moment with something amazing. Children have activities coming out of their ears, and the one thing they often lack is the chance to use their imagination and simply *play*. By giving them that kind of freedom, you're helping them discover themselves and develop in all kinds of ways.

Expanding Their Horizons

The time you spend with your grandchildren can be a useful counterbalance in their lives. Fern lives in a village with her husband, Colin, and two boys, Oz and Alex, who are fourteen and eleven. 'My mum doesn't live all that far away, but she's in the centre of Manchester, so when the kids go to stay, they get taken to restaurants, theatres, classical and pop concerts – it's a much more worldly experience than at home, and the contrast is good for them. They feel very sophisticated doing those things.'

This widening of experience can work the other way too. Rebecca and Owen discovered this with their grandchildren, four-year-old twins Casey and Corey. Rebecca says, 'We knew they hadn't had any experience with animals – you don't get much exposure to cows and piglets in central London, where they live. So we took them to a local petting zoo. They were keen to go, thrilled to see the little furry animals in the pens, and when we suggested we all get in with them, they said yes straight away. They were a bit tentative, but we persuaded them to pat a guinea pig or two, and then one of those giant rabbits came bounding up to Corey. She shrieked and ran right up me – I was practically wearing her like a hat! It took a while and a few trips, but nowadays they're much more blasé and relaxed with animals. We're sure it's done them good.'

Leroy and Sadie have used their granddaughters' visits to introduce them to the great outdoors. Sadie says:

> The girls are all city children, and although their parents work very hard to give them plenty of fresh air and do outdoorsy things like cycling and so on, with the best will in the world, it can be difficult to be spontaneous in a big town – getting on a bike means going to the park, and they have a small garden so there's not much scope there either. We try to compensate for this. We've got a big garden, complete with ponds, fish, stream, wild area, swing – a paradise for kids, you'd think. But when they were small, the girls were very *girly*. We'd send them out to play, togged up in their wellies and warm coats, but after about five minutes they'd be back inside. Our generation was used to ranging the fields in all weathers; playing out, not playing in was what you did. But even in the summer, our granddaughters were hard to keep outdoors for very long unless it was warm enough for the paddling pool.
>
> Maisie, the five-year-old, was standing next to me on the patio, and she said, 'What you need, Grandma, is more *stuff*.' She swept her arm round like a film director and said, 'You know – like a pink Wendy house and a trampoline, and a slide.' They've got plenty of intelligence and imagination – they read fantastically well and love books, and they've always been able to make up imaginary games – *inside*. They just weren't used to playing outside without 'stuff'.
>
> They're a bit older now, and gradually they've discovered the joys of being outdoors. We got them a toy kitchen, but they play with it outside. They commandeer the patio, litter

it with bits of cut-up carrot and potato, and pick my herbs, playing at restaurants. They write elaborate menus and don the aprons I made them, pretending to be chefs and wait-resses. We're the customers. We send them on adventures too – 'bear hunts' in the wild part of the garden beyond the stream. They draw complicated maps and I pack them some rations to take on their exploration. But there's a seat that's only about twenty feet down the garden, and they never get past that without stopping to eat everything in their bags. We watch them setting off and it's hilarious.

I made them some very basic flower-fairy costumes out of squares of coloured net, with bows pinned on their backs like wings, and they flit around the garden being 'invisible' by standing next to flowers that are the same shade. It's the only time I ever see them standing still and silent – and they can do it for a surprisingly long time. You'd have fun writing the think bubbles that go with their expressions. They're living out all kinds of stories in their heads.

Sadie and Leroy realise that children don't need elabo-rate toys to have fun. Once you set them off thinking in a new way they can enjoy all kinds of things. And it's amazing how little will please a child if it's done with love. Mavis and Gilbert make up kits for their grandchildren as presents. 'Instead of buying them something fancy and expensive, we might put together a collection of things that suit the temperament and interests of each child. When our grand-children were small they all loved washing things so we made up parcels with a small washing-up bowl, a dishcloth, tea-towel, dish mop and a little apron. They loved it. Or we'd do one with a plastic mixing bowl, wooden spoon, wire whisk, measuring cup, rolling pin and so on. Both boys and girls enjoy all that and they'll play for ages. We've made gardening kits, with a little trowel, gloves, fork, basket and packets of seeds, and craft kits with coloured paper, paints, apron, gauntlets, glue, glitter, stickers. You can do anything – it all depends on what your grandchildren enjoy.' Mavis and Gilbert are on to something here. Role-playing is a major way for children to learn.

Barty knows this from first-hand experience. He has two daughters, who often stay with his parents. 'When I was little my grandma made us try new things. We'd all have to do something different every day – maybe move some plants in the garden, clean a room, go shopping – even sew. And each thing we did, she'd talk about it with us, so we'd get some insight into how and why it was done that way – things to watch out for and so on. I learned an awful lot from that. Not just facts, but an understanding of how the world works. It was marvellous, and my parents try to do it for my daughters too.'

There's a lot to be said for this. It's one area where you can provide them with something that their parents won't – partly because of time, partly because of experience. Because you were brought up in a different world to your children, you have knowledge and memories of things they don't – and a captive audience. You can teach them different skills, too. Ernest has four great-grandchildren. He was a carpenter before he retired and still works with wood. 'My great-grandsons all want to spend time in my workshop. It fascinates them, and they always want to make something before they leave. So we do. However simple it is, they never go home empty-handed, and they're so proud of their effort.' This is a wonderful way to help children think three-dimensionally and develop physical dexterity – but educational jargon aside, it's just *fun* and gives them a sense of achievement and a feel for natural things.

Even if your particular skill is one their parents share, you still occupy a special place, as Connie found out. 'I've played the piano for years and my granddaughter is ten and learning too. Her father can play well, and he helps her with it, of course, but she still comes to me. She doesn't want me to teach her – she wants to show me what *she* can do. You've got to let children have the room to manoeuvre, not over-correct them.' It all comes back to letting them breathe – and do things for themselves. Lesley's got a sure-fire way – he has an electric train set, and his grandson Stuart loves it. 'Trains have been a hobby of mine for many years, and I have a model railway in the shed. Stuart was around five when I first let him play with it – change the points and so on. He was absolutely awestruck. He said, "Granddad, this is the best day of my life."'

There you have it in a nutshell – the magic of being a grandparent. And it comes in other ways – their beams of pleasure when they 'help' you with chores like sweeping the garden path (spreading the muck in every direction); or when they 'clean' the car, soaking themselves and everything else for yards around, leaving the vehicle itself looking more streaky and dirtier than it did to start with.

But it's all part of the relationship you share. Precisely because you're not their parents, you have a slight aura of mystery, of otherness, that gives you credibility in strange ways. Betty has five grandchildren, who range in age from nine to two. 'It's noticeable how both the boys and the girls go through similar stages – like believing in magic. Of course, with the boys it's dragons and monsters, and with the girls it's fairies. But they've all asked, at some time, whether there really *is* magic. They reach that moment when reality kicks in and starts to spoil things. I always tell them the same thing – that there's a little bit of magic in everybody; it's what makes us all special. I'm not trying to kid them – I think it's true, and

I want them to grow up knowing that the world is an amazing place — that there's room for more than just the prosaic.'

The fact is, children have an incredibly powerful imagination, and you're in the perfect position to feed it and help it grow.

Expanding *Your* Horizons

It's not just your grandchildren's horizons that widen — you'll find yours do too.

Whether it's rediscovering the joys of the rollercoaster, or inventing silly games to play on rainy days, you'll be stretched, as Alison is finding.

I have five grandchildren under ten, and they love me to make up stories, songs and poems for them at bedtime. That's all very well with the younger ones, who are only two, but the older ones are very well read and need proper plots — it can get quite tricky. I make them up as I go along and it's fine, but sometimes I get stuck part-way. Then, to give me time to come up with an ending, I have to tell them that I'll finish the story the next night. Phew! I might work in things they've done, either with us or with their parents, and sometimes I make the characters recognisable as the kids themselves — that always gets them going! I don't preach, or turn them into Victorian-style homilies, but I can see it makes them think.

Relating stories to the things your grandchildren have been up to, is a painless way to widen their perspective on the way they behave. It's good to recount tales of their ancestors too; funny, interesting, sometimes even sad stories about people they've never met, but whose photos they can find in your albums. It's history brought to life through people they're connected with, so it's imaginable – and *true*. You can start when they're small with simple stories about their parents, but these chunks of the past can be slanted to suit any age group – even teenagers (see Chapter 8).

There's really no end to these possibilities. Whatever your talents, you can depend on your grandchildren to be your biggest fans. Alastair has gained something of a reputation as a fixer with his grandchildren. 'I'm a practical person and, I suppose that over the years of DIY and so on, I've gained a fair bit of knowledge of how to mend things. So when the kids need a repair – anything from a loose nut on a bike to a missing wheel on a cart, it's me they come to – "Granddad, you can fix *anything*," they say, walking towards me with a handful of bits. So far it's been true, mostly – I only hope it stays that way!' Alastair's wife, Libby, has got a similar reputa-tion, but in a different field. 'I make dressing-up clothes for my grandchildren. I usually try to make them all a costume each for Christmas so that, as they grow out of them, there's a constant supply for younger siblings. It's great fun, but it can be a bit taxing if you're busy. Last year I made five major outfits – Belle, Cinderella, an Edwardian something from *The Railway Children* and two (more) fairies. They need to be hard-wearing – it's no good making something that falls apart, or that you have to follow them round and worry about – it has to be child-proof. I was sewing like mad right up to the wire. Still, the anticipation on their faces as they look under the tree – they expect them now – makes it all worth it.'

You don't need to be Schiapparelli to conjure up the odd costume for your grandchild – a pirate, say, might only need an ancient shirt, one of your old scarves, a belt and an eye-patch – it's the fact that you provided it that counts. And these days, every high street has several charity shops where you can find threadbare feather boas for next to nothing, along with ancient net underskirts and even cast-off commercial fancy-dress costumes. If you start collecting things and keep them in a box, there will always be a rainy-day alternative to the ubiquitous DVD or computer game. Dressing up isn't something only girls like, boys love it too – they just need someone to kick off the idea. And it doesn't all have to be fairy tales and princesses – space travel, monsters, jungles, survival and dinosaurs – are all fertile areas for generating enthusiasm in both sexes. It might mean re-stocking your house with things you thought you'd seen the last of decades ago, but what the heck? Cassie, grandmother of three, says, 'They love to come here. They take us for granted and that's how it should be. If I don't see them for a month I get miserable.'

The Christmas Issue

One thing that can change fundamentally when you have grandchildren, is Christmas. Not just how you spend it, but *where* you spend it. In many families, the arrival of grandchildren can effectively signal the end of the older generation hosting Christmas. The new mum makes a takeover bid, and grandparents are relegated to the role of guest/observer/ general dogsbody. This can apply whatever the major festival in your particular cultural life – suddenly there's a pretender to the throne.

Of course, you may be panting to hand over the sprout-bashing and turkey wrestling of the most stressful meal in the year to somebody (anybody) else. But, on the other hand, you might not be quite ready to relinquish your role at the heart of the family, in order to sit on the sidelines sipping sherry.

Over and above any religious significance, Christmas, like Hanukah, Chinese new year, Eid, Diwali and so on, provides an opportunity for families to get together to celebrate *being* a family. It's more than important, it's pivotal and, so, therefore, is the issue of who presides over it. It might always have been you. Every year, since what seems like the dawn of time, you've dusted off the decorations, bought staggering quantities of food, cooked up a storm and gathered your family to your bosom. Parting with that magic moment – the eye in the storm of the year – can be like losing your identity. In fact, you *are* losing it, or a part of it.

There are plenty of reasons why you won't want to; why this role is precious. For one thing, it's a sign you're still key figures in your family drama; you can put off thoughts of being 'past it' for a few years yet – you're not really middle-aged or, perish the thought, elderly. For another, it means you can still control events – you can do it *your* way – as an offering of love to those who love you.

That's about pride (albeit in a good, or at least understandable, way), but there are other, simpler, reasons, like the sheer joy of having all your children back in the nest; it's a parent thing, a nurturing instinct that's there for life. And you want to share the magic with your grandchildren – experience their wonder. Gradually, as your own children have grown older and stopped believing in Father Christmas, that magic has faded to more adult – and therefore less exciting – pleasures. You want, once again, to see Christmas through the eyes of a child. It brings back the magic for *you*, too.

But while you might be resisting the move into a less appealing phase, your children are doing the opposite – stepping further into adulthood. Once they have babies of their own, they stand where you found yourself a generation ago, at the head of a family. The role carries responsibilities and privileges, and one of those tends to be ownership of Christmas. Add to all this the fact that there could be another set of grandparents to factor in, equally keen, and with just as much right as you to be involved, and you have a potential recipe for stress and anxiety, if not anger and a little jealousy.

So before you start to let these feelings in, if your children say they want to 'do' Christmas, try to remember it's not about usurping *you* (although it might feel like that). It's about creating for their children, the stability and unity you created for them.

Elaine's daughter Eve and her partner, Ken, have eight-year-old triplets. Elaine says, 'When our grandchildren were five, Eve said she'd be happy to come to us, or Ken's mum, for Christmas Day, but whatever happened, she wanted to be at home for Christmas Eve. She said she had such great memories of Christmas Eve when *she* was a child – all the little traditions we had – and she and Ken wanted to develop their own so the children will have good memories when *they* grow up. I think she's dead right, and I'm glad she feels like that about her childhood.' Elaine is happy her daughter is establishing this continuity, but if you're feeling a bit hard done by, try not to get defensive, or angry, or, worse, self-pitying. It's best to face it – you're going to have to let go to a certain extent. And that's right, after all, you took over in your day, didn't you?

It doesn't necessarily mean you have to become a nonentity. Edna was very happy when her daughter Priscilla started to do Christmas. 'Priscilla was a bit over tactful, she seemed to think I might mind, but I was thrilled to bits. I mean, the thought of not having to worry about gravy or juggling roast potatoes . . . Instead of doing all those chores I'd be getting to play with my grandchildren – well, it was a no-brainer! As it turns out, of course, I never actually *do* get a long leisurely morning with the children. I'm in and out of the kitchen giving Priscilla a hand – peeling potatoes – whatever she needs to give *her* time for some fun too. I don't try to muscle in, just offer to help and when she wants me, I'm there. I don't feel I'm past my sell-by date. It's the best of both worlds, really.'

The revolution might not happen straight away, in any case. The first rumblings of independence tend to come when a baby is about two – able, in other words, to understand some of what's going on, to begin to appreciate the basics of whatever religious/philosophical background parents care to impart, the concept of Father Christmas, the decorations, and so on.

When Sarah and Brad had their first daughter, Ffion, they decided to carry on having Christmas with both their parents on alternate years, as they'd been doing since they married. Sarah says:

> I couldn't face the idea of doing all that work with a young baby – it made much more sense to carry on as normal. When our second daughter was born we did the same, until she reached about eighteen months. At that point we wanted to make Christmas for our children at home, and Brad and I both told our parents so. They were fine about it. Mum just said she didn't want to feel she'd *never* do it again – that she'd still like to have a year every now and then – and we make sure that happens. We have three children now, and our eldest is nine. My brother has two children in the same age group, and the families and grandparents sort of mix it up. Some years I'll have it for everybody, other years, my brother and his wife do it, and sometimes one or other – or all of us, will spend it with either of our parents. It works because all the various grandparents are with at least one set

of their children every year as hosts or as guests. Everyone gets a turn. We're all very flexible.

This is a good arrangement – no one has annexed Christmas, and so no one feels as though they're being left out – or dumped on, for that matter. Even though Sarah and Brad live at a distance from both sets of parents, they haven't let this stop them from doing what suits everyone. When families don't get on, it can be more difficult.

Bret and Eileen don't spend Christmas with her parents. Eileen says, 'I never enjoyed Christmas at home as a kid – it was always tense. Mum rushed around and Dad would lose his temper. We always had my auntie and grandma round for dinner and I can't remember a year when there wasn't a row of some kind. And it was so boring – I used to dread it. Bret hasn't got any family, so when we had our two boys we leapt at the excuse to have Christmas at home. Mum was furious. We fought about it. These days we just pop in on Christmas Eve for an hour so they can give the kids some presents – get it over with.' This is such a shame – everybody's missing out here. But it's never too late to mend fences. Whatever your situation, the best way to resolve it is always to talk to each other. Try not to fall out, but there's absolutely no point in bottling it up as long as you approach it calmly. Your family might not even realise what you're feeling, and a quiet word could transform the situation.

If things do become fraught, remember that it's about the children, rather than individual egos or grouches – yours or any of your family's. Tempers often rise at Christmas anyway: it's the classic time for tears over the stove, because of the pressure to make everything perfect. Forget perfect – children don't notice if the gravy's lumpy – but they do notice tension.

Stanley and Ellen live very near all their thirteen grand-children, so the whole Christmas experience is very relaxed. 'Ellen and I have made it a point not to hang on to Christmas,' says Stanley. 'All the family gets a go and we do it differ-ently every year. We want it to be inclusive. One year we hired the village hall so everyone could be together at once – it's a lot of people! It was great because our grandchil-dren did a "panto" on the stage for all the grown-ups after lunch! We do have traditions, though. Every year Ellen and I throw a Christmas party just for the children and Ellen reads *The Night Before Christmas*. They all like that – even the older ones.'

It doesn't matter whether the things you do are small or large scale – what counts is that they're special to your family. Ambrose and Flora started traditions that their children still carry on with their own. Flora recalls:

When the kids were very small, we thought we'd try to prevent those crack-of-dawn present-opening orgies, where everything's peaked before breakfast. We wanted to stretch out the fun. So on Christmas Eve, we'd tell them that Santa would leave their presents and stockings downstairs, but that when they woke up, they didn't need to go down to check – they'd know he'd been because he'd have left them loads of balloons in their rooms, and they could play with them until Mummy and Daddy woke up. It worked like a charm. Every year, last thing before we went to bed, we'd blow up a couple of packs of balloons and waft them into the children's bedrooms. We'd stagger up the stairs giggling (it's amazing how difficult it is to herd large numbers of balloons) and, incredibly, none of them ever woke up to see us doing it. In the morning we'd hear their voices saying 'He's been!' and it gave us time to make a cup of tea and get some clothes on. Now some of our grandchildren do that. It's part of Christmas.

Talking about childhood Christmases can be a good way to regenerate old ideas and come up with new ones. But if your children want to break away from what you did, try to understand. This is *their* shot at it.

It's not only Christmas – family festivals are the jewels in the crown, so why not invite everyone for Easter, or some other milestone moment in your cultural year? And if you don't have one – invent one. Pick a weekend – make the third weekend in September, or the second weekend in February, the one when all the family comes together at your place – everyone knows, it's in their diaries every year, so they plan round it. Take family photos with the full line-up, frame them and hang them on the wall. Your grandchildren will love looking at them – now and long after you're gone. Magic.

HOW TO GET THE BALL ROLLING

Try Saying

Do you need a break – shall we babysit for a couple of hours?

Do you fancy a night out? We could stay at your place overnight.

Take a weekend – spoil yourselves – you can leave the
· children with us.

If you want to do some decorating/gardening/whatever, we'll
have the kids.

How about giving the kids a week with us at half term/in the
summer holidays?

KEEPING THEM IN LINE

Don't

Tell on them to their parents once you've disciplined them.

Make them follow a lot of new rules.

Undermine their parents.

Do

Make sure you know what their parents' rules are.

Discuss them and agree on an approach for when the children
are with you.

Stick to what you've agreed – be consistent.

WINNING THE FOOD WARS

Relax – don't try to reform their eating habits completely.

Help them to enjoy new food experiences.

Make it fun.

Try one new food at a time.

Make it look tempting.

Let them help you cook it.

Treat them like grown-ups.

Be flexible.

Let them make choices.

HAVING A HAPPY CHRISTMAS

Don't	**Do**
Say 'I *always* do Christmas'.	Say 'I'd like to have it some years – can we keep it flexible?'
Say 'I'll show you how to do it.'	Say 'If you need any help or information – just ask.'
Breeze in and take over, or breathe down their necks.	Offer to help with the chores.

5

Taking Care of Your Grandchildren

It's well known that childcare provision in the UK lags behind the rest of Europe: there isn't enough of it and what there is is patchy. Local-authority nurseries are in very short supply, while childminders and privately run nurseries have waiting lists, enabling them to command substantial fees, particularly the better ones. Unlike many European businesses, very few UK companies choose to invest in their employees by providing a crèche, leaving them to juggle their work and family commitments. No one wins.

A lot of couples with young children choose to work, but there are also many who *have* to work full-time, just to pay their mortgage or rent. The increase in divorce and relationship breakdowns means there are more single parents than ever before working their socks off trying to make ends meet.

But here comes the cavalry – grandparents galloping to the rescue. It's estimated that 60 per cent of childcare in the UK is provided by grandparents and nationally the savings to parents is billions of pounds. Hooray!

Except it's not quite as simple as that – things rarely are. On the plus side, what could be more wonderful than young children being nurtured and cared for by the second most important people in their lives? They benefit hugely in a thousand ways: they love their grandparents, feel comfortable, happy, relaxed and secure. Parents feel they can trust *their* parents completely, so they relax too. And grandparents? They get what most grandparents want: extensive access to their grandchildren. It all helps to bind families together in a shifting society, and harks back to the good old days of everyone in the family having a role in a fully functioning mutual support system. So all's well in a perfect world? Not necessarily.

We might be the youngest, fittest, most active grandparents in history but, partly because of that, we're also retiring much later. And the high divorce rate applies to us too, so at a time when we might have thought our mortgage would be paid off, and we'd happily be squirreling away cash for our old age, we could still be making those monthly payments – with the end nowhere in sight. What's more, UK provision for the elderly isn't that great, and we're all living much longer, so we'll *need* that money. Oh yes, and the fact that people are living longer means that their own parents might still be alive, and a drain on time, energy, and emotions . . .

So, helping with the care of your grandchildren can pose at least some of the same kinds of problems for you as it does for their parents. Even if you're retired, comfortably off, and raring to go, there are a lot of factors to take into consideration: where you live relative to your children, your long-term health, for example. Still, we're hard-wired to help our children. If they have a problem of any kind, we'll stretch ourselves to give them a hand. We're equally programmed to be there for our grandchildren, even to the point of taking over the role of parent should that be necessary. We count ourselves lucky to be there for our family. And they're lucky, too, that we are.

Talking About It

If your children ask you for help with childcare, whether it's a little or a lot, it can be very tempting to say 'yes' immediately, but it's important to think it through, and then discuss things with them before you decide. This isn't being difficult, it's being sensible; if you anticipate problems, you can solve them up front.

Of course, in the process, you may realise it's impossible for you to do it at all – but it's far better to make that discovery before you've actually begun, than to have to drop it midstream, something that can result in disagreements, inconvenience for everyone and disappointment for your grandchildren. This happened to Marie and Sid. Their son Derek with his wife and two sons, live eight miles away. Sid recalls:

> Cody's five and at infants' school, and Ross is two and goes to nursery. Derek works long hours, so our daughter-in-law Julie always did the school runs because she worked locally. Then she was offered a job a few miles away on the other

side of their town, so they asked us if we'd do the teatime school run for them. It didn't sound like much, and we're both retired, so we agreed. It meant Julie could take the job, and we liked the idea of spending an hour or so with the boys every afternoon, but it turned out to be a nightmare. It's only a few miles from us to them, but the traffic's awful, and we had to set off really early to be sure of getting there for half past three, because Cody wasn't signed on for after-school club – his mum and dad don't approve of it – and we couldn't leave him stranded. It did happen a couple of times at first, and his teacher was very offhand with us – you can't blame her, but it felt as if we were neglecting him.

Ross was OK until six o'clock, but we couldn't be late for him, either, because they fine you a fiver for every five minutes you're late. We'd take Cody back to their parents' house, give him his tea and play with him, then I'd go to fetch Ross. It was often getting on for seven by the time their mum got in, and then we'd have to get in the car and drive all the way home.

Don't get me wrong; we loved being with the boys. Just seeing their faces when we went to pick them up was worth the hassle, but after a while it began to take its toll. They're lovely kids, but they're typical boys, and hard work. We're reasonably fit, but we're both seventy and we were getting very tired. The stress of driving against the clock was wearing, too. And it was taking up a lot more of our day than we'd thought it would. We'd leave the house at around two thirty and never be home before half past seven. Then Marie would cook supper, and it would be time for bed. Our own lives had somehow got lost in all the rush – and we didn't have much energy left for anything else, anyway. Still, we kept on, because we knew they'd struggle without us.

It all blew up when we told them we were planning to go off to Portugal for a couple of weeks – we have a holiday with our friends most years. We were giving them lots of warning, but straightaway Julie said, 'But what about the boys?' As if they were all *our* responsibility! I'm afraid I lost my temper then. I said they'd forgotten we had lives too; that they were taking us for granted. They accused us of being selfish. It was outrageous after all we'd done! That was the end of it as far as I was concerned. I told them they'd have to make other arrangements. I know Marie would have weakened if I'd let her, but I wouldn't cave in. We carried on until Julie fixed something up locally with another mum.

We didn't see them for a bit after that, and we missed the boys a lot. But it couldn't have gone on, even if it hadn't all erupted. We were running ourselves ragged, and Julie and Derek didn't seem to appreciate it at all. Things have warmed up again now, but I'm sure Julie still thinks we let them down.

This is such a pity but, given the circumstances, it was an argument waiting to happen. Marie and Sid were at the end of their tether and, because of that, ripe for a fight. Derek and Julie panicked at the thought of the childcare unravelling, and said things they didn't mean. It might all have been avoided if, before they said yes, Marie and Sid had really thought about what it would involve. Naturally they were keen to do it, so they didn't consider there might be drawbacks. They hadn't remembered how tiring young children can be and, in any case, the traffic, location, timing equation made it a huge task. If they'd discussed all that with their children, it might have been possible to find another way – perhaps they could have done it a couple of times a week instead of every day. Or maybe Julie and Derek would have reconsidered after-school club for Cody, which would have meant they could both have been picked up later. Another option would have been to say no – gently but firmly – explaining they'd have loved to do it, but laying out what the difficulties were. It's likely Derek and Julie simply didn't realise what hard work it would be.

It's hard to refuse your children, but sometimes you have to be strong. Norman and Virginia are prepared for that if necessary. Their daughter Charmaine has a new baby boy. Norman explains: 'Charmaine hasn't gone back to work yet. When she does, I think she'll want us to look after our grandson – but we're not going to do five days a week. Virginia isn't well enough, and the lifting would be too much for her. In any case, I'm semi-retired, and we might move to the south coast when I finish working; I think we've earned a rest. We'd still see a lot of them, because they'd come down for holidays and weekends. But we wouldn't move just to avoid helping. If we stay here, when the time comes, we'll be quite happy to tell them we can't do it and why. I expect we could cover it, together with his other grandma, but we wouldn't want to do it all.'

It's best to be straightforward about this. There's no reason to feel guilty about voicing your legitimate concerns. And what if you simply don't fancy the idea? Well, that's OK too – you're adults, with the right to a life of your own – there's no rule that says 'good' grandparents have to sacrifice all their time and reorganise their lives to suit their children. Whatever your view, it's best to explain how you feel – don't get defensive – just be honest. You might find you've been worrying for no reason. But you'll never know if you don't tell them the truth.

Some grandparents find other ways of helping. Doreen and Fraser's daughter Gemma was widowed when her son Gavin was eighteen months old. Fraser remembers: 'Gemma couldn't afford a nursery for Gavin – they cost a fortune and she just didn't earn enough. Doreen and I couldn't have him because we're still working, so we offered to pay nursery fees for him. We've paid off our mortgage, so we had enough spare cash, just. At first Gemma said no, she wouldn't accept it because it was a lot of money, and we'd be paying for several years. So we compromised. We pay just over half, which means Gemma can manage the rest. She doesn't feel so bad about that, and it's not as much of a strain on us, either. It's made us poorer, but she's our daughter – we're glad to do it.' Doreen and Fraser's solution was possible for them because they were still working. Many grandparents wouldn't have sufficient disposable income to do this, but an increasing number have some financial input into their grandchildren's nursery fees.

Getting What You All Want

It's very, very easy for resentments to build up, bubble under the surface, and then break out in rows that can split families apart, sometimes for years. One of the main reasons this happens is that people don't talk to each other about big – or small – things. Sitting down together, not just to explain how you feel, but to *listen* and really hear what others are saying can transform a situation because you start to see things from the other person's point of view.

Your children might be asking for anything from full-on childcare to a one day a week pick-up from nursery or school, but whatever the level of commitment, if you work out all the pros and cons, all the possible glitches and hitches, you can address them together and you're more likely to come to an arrangement which will please everyone and be sustainable. But you have to work out what the difficulties are, and this means looking at everything in depth.

So first, discuss every conceivable aspect with your partner. Ask yourselves how you *really* feel about it (and don't assume you already know how your partner feels – you might be surprised). How often would you feel happy helping – as often as they want you to do it? What about the physical arrangements – do they involve a lot of driving or rushing about? Are you up for that? Can you afford it? It's perfectly reasonable to ask for expenses. And your children might well not think of that, left to themselves. What effect would the proposed arrangement have on your own life? Would it fit in with your work? Would you have time to carry on with your own interests? Do you think it would be fun – would you enjoy it?

Of course, circumstances can change. When Norah and Perry's first grandson was born, Norah volunteered to look after him for one day a week.

I'd been planning to stop work anyway, and spending one day every week with my grandson was nice. When his sisters were born I carried on – I even taught them all to read. It was a good arrangement for everyone. In fact it still is. The children are twelve, nine and six now, and we still have them one day a week after school.

When our other daughter, Astrid, had her fourth baby, they moved to be near to us. She was at home with the children, but she knew she'd need a bit of back-up now and then, because her husband worked really long, unsocial hours, and he was never there.

Then, three years ago, they split up, and Astrid got a job. Perry and I took on getting *her* four children off to school, and picking them up in the afternoon. And that's what we do. Four days a week, we go to their house, give them breakfast, take them to school, and then pick them up at three thirty and give them their tea here. Their mum comes for them at six. And on the fifth day, we still have our eldest daughter's children – no free time for us.

I can't say it's what we want, but there's no alterna-tive – I really don't see what we could do to change it. The children need the stability of knowing that it's always Mummy or Granny who's going to be at the school gate, not some unknown childminder – and Astrid can't afford to pay someone anyway. My husband doesn't like it that I'm so busy all the time, but we volunteered. We couldn't have let her struggle. It's hard to go it alone with four children under six. Astrid knew I was here and could help her. It was a nightmare when they were all in preschool – exhausting – but we managed. We never have a real holiday, although we do take the children away – otherwise they wouldn't get one. It will be easier as they get older, but it's an unrelenting routine. We try to babysit, too – Astrid is lonely – she needs a life as well. We can cope in term time, but the school holidays are very tiring. And what would we do if I was ill? There's no back-up – we live from day to day.

I don't think Astrid realises we worry about all this. She thinks, well, we love the children – and of course we do – but our whole life is on hold. I don't want to be getting up at six thirty in the morning for ever. And Perry wants to retire, but he can't – he's financial back-up for Astrid. She can cope, just, but she has no money in the bank.

On the up side, we have a really close relationship with our grandchildren. We're very careful not to upstage their mum, but we're a big influence on them – we help with their homework and so on. And we're *lucky* – we know people who'd give anything to have what we have – all these very different, loving grandchildren around us all the time.

We're glad to do it, really – a child is better with someone who loves it. I'd hate it if they lived a long way off and we were just acquaintances.

Events overtook Norah and Perry and changed their plans radically. They're doing wonders, and their daughter appreciates it – but Norah's right to worry about the health factor. However much you won't want to admit it, having young children around in your sixties is much harder work than when you're younger, and long term it can be a strain.

So that's another major question to ask yourself – are you fit enough to do it? Be honest – no wishful thinking. Your children, however much they might need help, really wouldn't want you to make yourselves ill. But they won't necessarily know just how fit you are. We all tend to imagine our parents will last for ever; we don't like to think of them getting old. In other words, you might not be the only ones prone to wishful thinking. That means you need to know your limitations.

Noel and Sheena were in their seventies when their granddaughter Pia was born. Noel recalls: 'Our daughter Marjorie was going back to work after six months, and we offered to look after Pia, because we didn't like the idea of her going to a nursery before she was one. It worked well, but we had to cut it a bit short, because Sheena developed sciatica. When Pia's sister Donna was born, we did the same, but it was physically harder. By then we weren't so fit, and we had to bring the playroom downstairs. There's a lot to looking after babies – it's effectively eleven hours a day: keeping them amused and entertained, running round after them, pushing the pram to the shops or the park . . . And then you have to use the weekends to catch up on your own chores.'

Sheena says, 'Of course we enjoyed it. We'd talk to them,

sing songs – Noel even put the rudiments of potty training in place before they each left us. But he had to take them out for a while during the day, to give me a break. We'd go to pick up the baby, and watch Marjorie running for the bus. We admire our daughter so much. Young people work hard these days – life is tough. We were glad to help. We still do, when they need us.'

Marjorie and her husband, Jerry, understood completely. Jerry remembers: 'It had never occurred to us they'd want to look after Pia – we'd booked a nursery place for her. When they offered we were surprised and absolutely delighted. We cancelled the nursery and bought some equipment – a cot and so on. It was lovely for Pia to have the benefit of one-to-one care with her own family, and it saved us money too. But when Sheena's sciatica began, it was clear she wouldn't be able to carry a baby around. So we went back to the nursery, and said – "You know that place we didn't want . . ." When they said they'd do it with Donna too, we were pleased but a bit worried about them. Donna was a bigger, heavier baby and very mobile – she walked before she was twelve months old, and they had to stop looking after her at that point.' It all worked out because Marjorie and Jerry didn't take Sheena and Noel for granted, and were watching carefully to see that they were coping. But you need to do this for yourself, too.

You may be bouncing with health like the dogs in the vitamin adverts, but be realistic – that touch of arthritis or tendency to back pain could turn out to be a real drag when you're lifting heavy infants or toddlers on and off chairs, or bending to fasten shoes and pull up pants . . . And think of that 'liquid baby' thing they do, when you try to pick them up and they resist you, flop down and seem to be glued to the floor – it's guaranteed to wreck your lower back.

So, if you go ahead, pace yourself. Try to arrange some

respite – perhaps network with their friends' mums or grandparents and see if you can fix something up, especially if
you're a single grandparent. It worked when you were a
young family – why not now? When you're part of a couple
it's a bit easier – you can give each other a break, and tackle
the things that best suit each of you and your health. It's
fun to take a toddler to the park, for example, but pushing
a swing is one thing, holding on to a two-wheeled bicycle
while a child learns to balance is something else altogether.

This isn't to say that you should retire to your bath chair
immediately, just don't try to do everything their parents do
– it will wear you to a shred. It's easy to be blasé, especially if
you already enjoy taking your grandchildren on very active
holidays – but then you can hand them back and put your
feet up. Looking after energetic youngsters month in, month
out, is a different matter. You might be the sexiest sixty-year-
old on the block, but time has a way of marching on.

If there's another set of grandparents, and they're available,
consider sharing the task between you. This isn't just about
spreading the labour – jealousy can rear its ugly head. How
would you feel if the other set were asked and you weren't?
Left out? Passed over? Not so loved or trusted? Would you
wonder if they thought you weren't capable? It can be well
worth both couples getting together and working out a
proposal which you can put to your children and refine to
suit you all.

It's not just grandparents who can become jealous, as Beryl
and Archie discovered. Archie says, 'When our daughter went
back to work, we spent a year looking after her twin girls,
and our son got very disgruntled. He kept saying "Those kids
are always here – you don't see enough of mine." It's true
they were a handful and took up a lot of time, but he didn't
get over it until they went to nursery. We tried to be fair to

his two sons, who are older, but there wasn't enough time to go round.'

This is another situation where a chat can work wonders. If Archie and Beryl had explained that they were trying their best, and didn't have favourites, it might have calmed their son down. And they could have suggested things all the children could do together as cousins, which would have had the double bonus of helping them to bond, while giving Archie and Beryl the occasional break.

Childminding

If full-time childcare for under-school-age children is on your agenda, there's a lot to think about. For a start, where is it going to take place – in your house or theirs? There are pros and cons whichever you choose. Their parents might be happier to have you on the spot, rather than having to come and pick them up at the end of the day. Partly because if they're held up for any reason, you can put the children to bed; and all their toys, books, equipment and clothes will be handy, which will mean they – or you – won't have to drag mountains of kit backwards and forwards (and, incidentally, *your* house won't be trashed). You'll be ideally placed for babysitting too. On the minus side, it's you who will have to turn out at the crack of dawn to arrive before they leave for work – and it's you who will have to go out into the cold at the end of a tiring day. Unless you live round the corner and are in perfect health, this could be a big factor.

If you do the childminding at your house, you'll need to look at how safe it is for young children, and take steps to child-proof it. Stair gates, cupboard locks, fireguards and various other gadgets will appear on your horizon, and they need to be taken seriously. Is your house on a busy road? Do you have a secure fence and garden gate? A fishpond? A pet? Where do you keep your pills, bleach, scissors? Yes, you already have the children to visit and you take care, but that's not the same as them being with you every day of every week. If there are holes in your defences, they'll find them.

Whichever house you choose, it's best to lay down some ground rules for their parents about being home on time, and not dropping you in it too often by working late, or ringing at the last minute to ask if they can stay out for the evening. By all means be flexible, but don't be a doormat. If you're going to be such an intimate part of each other's lives, then there has to be some give and take and that means they have to do some of the giving, as well as the taking.

You'll need to agree about other things too: what happens if you're ill – what back-up will there be? What are you going to feed the children? If they're picky, or going through the terrible twos, it will be *you* who fights the food wars, not their parents, and you need to make sure you win them, or mealtimes will be one long conflict (see Chapters 3 and 4).

Which leads you neatly on to discipline (see Chapter 3). Children are programmed to be survivors – they're gifted opportunists, and will insert all their fingernails into any perceived cracks, however small, between you and their parents and rip everything apart. Talk to your children about how they want discipline dealt with, but don't hesitate to put your views too. In this case it definitely isn't interference. You'll be in charge of long stretches of their lives, and it's in everyone's interests – not least your grandchildren's – that you all feel happy about what's going down. Imagine a couple of rampaging toddlers, and your hands tied because you haven't agreed a strategy.

It's also a good idea, to give some thought to what the

children will be doing all day. When you're with them usually, it's for relatively short periods. Even if they stay with you for two weeks at a time, it's an event, and will have novelty value. But now, you're sacrificing your celebrity status to become routine – a lot of your starry advantages are about to evaporate like Cinderella's coach and horses at midnight. So you'll need a plan to give shape to their days. Try to avoid boredom by making every day a mix of environments and moods – strenuous outdoor play, noisy indoor fun, a sleep or quiet time, and periods for reading, painting, sticking, drawing, storytelling, listening to music, singing. The National Literacy Trust has a pack to help grandparents communicate with their grandchildren, and there are other organisations to help you (see page 261).

What you choose to do will depend on their age and interests, but whatever it is, it's best for them – and you – to keep it coming. Young children don't move seamlessly from one engrossing activity to the next, they dash headlong from one messy game to another, leaving chaos in their wake – chaos which *you* are going to be cleaning up before the next day's onslaught. (Teaching them to tidy up after themselves can be a rewarding thing to do.)

But if you're childminding at their house, a word of warning – don't be tempted to start wielding a duster, cleaning bathrooms or becoming unpaid housekeepers. You're only trying to help, but your children might take it as veiled criticism. You're not Mary Poppins – you can't wave a wand at it – it's extra work. Save your energy for the children; they'll take all of it, and more.

If this all sounds like organising a major military exercise, that's because it is. It doesn't mean it won't be great fun and wonderfully rewarding for all of you, but the more you plan it, the more rewarding it will be. There's serious research to show that grandparents have a highly positive and beneficial effect on their grandchildren in their intellectual, social *and* emotional development.

Making It Formal

Many grandparents take on childminding for love – their children might not be able to afford the commercial kind but, even if they could, it wouldn't occur to anyone to talk about money – it's a family thing. If that's how you all feel, then fine, but if your own financial situation means you do need to consider costs or payment for your time, then don't be afraid to say so.

There's no bar to your children giving you expenses but, legally, they can't pay you for the care itself unless you're officially registered as a childminder, in which case you have to look after at least one other child over and above your own grandchildren, and not do it in your grandchildren's home.

If parents are working over sixteen hours a week, then, subject to a means test, some can claim up to 80 per cent of the cost of childcare – but not if it's being provided by grandparents or other family members (including step-grandparents), unless they're registered childminders. This is called tax credit and, in principle, it applies right across the UK, but it's complex, the rules and criteria vary locally and are very subjective (see page 261).

If you want to become a registered childminder, you'll need to train and have your premises inspected for suitability by OFSTED. You'll also need public liability insurance, and a police check on you and anyone in your household over sixteen. Your local authority will have an Early Years Development and Childcare Partnership, and that's a good place to start (see page 260). It might sound like a bit of a faff, but the whole process only takes about three months, and can be a great way to help everyone, as Rita discovered. She has two grandchildren now aged five and six.

> When my daughter Val had her girls, she wanted to go back to work, but her pay wasn't much, and nurseries where they live cost an arm and a leg. She asked me to do it – but I was working part-time myself, and I didn't really want to give up. In fact, I couldn't afford to. But I could see Val and her boyfriend were having a hard time of it on the money front, and I thought – why not? I love kids, I'm pretty fit, and I might be able to turn it into a nice little home-based business. I got the training and set myself up. It worked like a dream. I looked after three other kids on top of my grandchildren, and I've carried on now they're at school. It's hard work, but it's so nice to spend the time with young children – they're lovely. It isn't a cash fountain, but it makes me enough money so I don't miss my old job – and I enjoy this much more. We all win. It's great.

Rita has made a new career, but she's fit and active. She needs to be – this is not a job for the frail. Once you're registered, there are start-up grants available, depending on your circumstances, and generous tax breaks for child-minders, so don't let lack of funds prevent you if you're keen. Remember, you'll be self-employed, and will need to pay National Insurance. You'll be running a business, so it's important to look at the market before you set your fees – but there's a lot of information out there to help you through (see page 261).

Coming to the Rescue

There are times when there isn't an opportunity to plan anything. An emergency happens and grandparents take over. Tara was hospitalised with an ectopic pregnancy, and her mother, Agnes, went to take care of eighteen-month-old Terry. 'I stayed for five days, but sadly, Tara lost the baby. Terry only partly understood what was going on, but I'd take him to visit his mum, and he'd cuddle her on the hospital bed. He was very independent, but he needed lots of love and hugs from me. You can make a child feel safe when frightening things happen just by keeping to his familiar routine and trying to do all the things his mummy would do. It brought us very close.'

Continuity is important to a child when things are going wrong, and that's the marvellous thing about grandparents – we can give them this. If something unusual is happening in their lives, even if it's not permanent or really very serious it can feel that way to children, and they can easily become insecure, even frightened. It's hard to explain things to the very young, so the constant, reliable presence of people they love will make all the difference and reinforce what their parents are saying.

When Freda's son Lance went into hospital, she reorganised her life for a while to help.

Lance went in as an emergency, and when my daughter-in-law rang to tell me, I asked if she'd like me to come and sort out the kids, who are four and two, for the duration. She works full-time, and rushes home to pick them up from school and nursery every night. I volunteered to stay, so I could get them off in the mornings, and then pick them up in the evenings, leaving her free to go straight to the hospital from work. I did it for several weeks until Lance came home. We settled into a routine − I'd go to them on Tuesday mornings and come home on Friday mornings so I had some time to catch up on commitments at home. My husband couldn't come with me, because he was at work.

Of course, I was glad to help. It seemed to me that with their dad not there, the children needed someone familiar and reassuring. It worked very well − their other grandparents did the Monday runs and Tuesday mornings, and my daughter and son-in-law collected them on Friday afternoons for supper and a sleepover with their cousins, so it was a real family affair!

Spreading the load in this way meant it could carry on for longer than if it had all fallen on one person. In this instance, the family is a close one and everyone was glad to chip in, but if your family isn't so accommodating, and an emergency happens, it's worth getting together and having a chat about it. If someone's reluctant to do their bit, try to keep your temper − don't accuse them of anything, or ask them to take on something you know would be very difficult for them. Instead, work out what would be possible for everyone, and allocate the tasks between you accordingly. Try to work together, so no one feels put on or resentful.

Sometimes the response needs to be for more than a few weeks; it can stretch to years. Nell and Blake's daughter Ceri was widowed when her first child, Abbie, was a baby, and they stepped in to care for her four days a week so Ceri could go back to work. Nell says:

I just thanked God I was retired and could do it. I had Abbie for four years, and it was a total joy. We made sure her other granddad saw her every week, too − that's very important – and she gets on well with him, but, probably because I've had her from a baby, she and I are so close, it's amazing. She's a shy child, but with me she laughs and chats away. I've been quite strict with her – maybe more so than her mum, and I've never had any trouble with discipline, not because she's an angel, but because she's so fond of me that she doesn't want to upset me, and if she's naughty she'll apologise straight away and give me a hug!

Ceri has a new partner now – a lovely man – and they've got an eight-month-old baby boy. We stopped looking after Abbie when he was born, because my daughter was on maternity leave. When we gave up, Abbie was quite worried. She said, 'But, Grandma, I am going to see you, aren't I?' We had to reassure her.

Blake suggested we retire to the coast, but I persuaded him to stay here; I couldn't go so far away. Now Ceri's going back to work so we'll start all over again, this time with both children, but only for two days a week. We'll have the baby all day, and pick Abbie up from school. I'm looking forward to getting back into the fray – I've missed Abbie so much, and I'm hoping to develop the same kind of relationship with her brother.

My other daughter has two girls, and although we all love each other a lot, I don't think the relationship is quite the same because we've never had to be involved in such a big way. Abbie has stayed overnight so often, and there's something about having a child when their mum's not around – you build such a fantastic rapport. I only hope it carries on as they grow older – I couldn't bear to lose them.

People say I do too much, but I enjoy it. Grandchildren keep you young – they're a gift.

Nell and Blake have been – and still are – a vital component in their grandchildren's lives. She doesn't need to worry that they'll drift away – the bond they've established will last for ever.

If the situation is likely to stretch over a long period like this, it can be worth looking at getting together with other grandparents and children. Grainne looks after her grandson Rory five days a week. 'I have two friends with grandchildren the same age as Rory, so every Friday we all meet up and do something – it might be swimming, or a theme park, a walk in the woods, a picnic. We go on buses, trains, whatever – and we never miss. It's great for all of us. The children have become good friends and they love it.' This means Grainne keeps in touch with her own friends, and the children get to spend time with others of their own age – something that would happen automatically if their parents were doing the childcare. It will give them lots of happy memories to look back on.

Meg and Wilfred have only memories of two of their granddaughters, who died aged six and seven of a rare genetic disorder. Meg says, 'We'd have them to stay with us to give them a change, and so their mum and dad could have a break. It was heartbreaking to watch them go downhill and become progressively less active. All we could do was be there for them, show them that they were loved. They'd sit on my knee, just twiddling my hair. In the end they became too ill to come to us – they needed twenty-four-hour care and had to move into a hospice. They fought like mad to survive, those girls. We celebrate their birthdays every year with balloons – they're still our granddaughters.' Meg and Wilfred did what they could to help their daughter and enhance their grand-daughters' lives. Whatever form childcare takes, whether it's for a few hours or five days a week, a one-off or it lasts for years, it all boils down to that in the end.

But sometimes, tragically, it can backfire, and that vital continuity can be compromised. This happened to Zelda.

My daughter Cressy was a single parent at nineteen. She had my grandson Louie as an emergency Caesarean, and when she got home from hospital, she found it hard to manage. My ex-husband and I did everything we could to help and support her and I often spent five days a week at her house, looking after them both. Sometimes I stayed overnight, and then at weekends I'd babysit. This went on for several years – I felt like Louie's second mum.

Then Cressy got a new partner and everything changed. I had a great bond with Louie – I didn't even have to tell him off – but my daughter would scream at him. It dawned on me that she was jealous and was punishing him for being fond of me. One day we had a row about it, and Louie said he wanted to come and live with me. He packed his own bag – he was only four. It was awful. It took me hours to calm everything down.

Then I got a solicitor's letter saying I wasn't allowed contact with Louie any more – that I'd never see him again. There were some trumped-up things about giving him fizzy drinks against her wishes and other nonsensical stuff. The letter said that if I wanted access, I'd have to go to court. I was beside myself, but I didn't try to get legal access. I know it can help in some cases, but I thought it might make things worse between us. And I was afraid that if I did, my grandson would suffer for it. In all, I thought it might do more harm than good.

I didn't see Louie for *three years*. Several times I arranged some mediation for Cressy and me, but she'd never turn up. I'd phone her and hear Louie screaming in the background, 'I want to see my nanny.'

When my sister came over from Australia to visit us, Cressy and I made up, but I had to get to know Louie all over again. I didn't know what he liked to eat, to read – anything. It all did Louie devastating damage. He was punished for wanting to see me, and told that he couldn't because he was naughty, so he feels guilty about what happened. I realise it was down to Cressy's jealousy – her way of controlling things.

My daughter did some serious thinking, and I've forgiven her. We're back on track – but it's always fragile. I tell Louie I love him, but I have to be extremely careful. I hold back from him a little bit in case Cressy gets jealous again. I don't want to be barred from seeing him – and I don't want him to suffer. Louie's nearly ten now, and some day I'll have to help him understand it wasn't his fault. I've seen the worst and best sides of being a grandparent, and the one thing I've learned is that you have to let people work through their own issues. One day, Louie will be able to make up his own mind.

Zelda's experience shows that it can sometimes be a fine line between bonding with your grandchild and upsetting your own child. If they're insecure or off-balance in any way because of what's going on in their own lives, your actions might be misinterpreted. That's not to say you shouldn't act, of course, but you may need to think carefully about what you do and how you do it. Talk to your child about what's happening, explain that you're not trying to upstage them. What Zelda and her family have been through is heartbreaking and far-reaching in its consequences for all of them. It highlights the fact that access is one of the many ways in which grandparents lack rights concerning their grandchildren (see pages 269–71 and Chapter 7).

Becoming Parents to Your Grandchildren

Some grandparents enter a completely different dimension. They don't just help out with the care of their grandchildren, they become full-time parents for the second time around. It's thought that over 200,000 grandparents in the UK are currently bringing up one or more grandchild under thirteen years of age. They do this in response to some dreadful family catastrophe, and it changes everything for ever. It may be the solution that provides their grandchildren with the equivalent of loving parents and a normal, secure life, but for grandparents it can come at an enormous cost in anxiety, stress and hard work. Those who do it say that the rewards far, far outweigh the drawbacks, but it's an heroic act, if for no other reason than the fact that you may well have to fight 'city hall' to make it happen in the first place. The system seems to be biased against grandparents.

Grandparents and the Law

There are laws and procedures but, as grandparents, you don't have *any* automatic rights – you must apply to the court, and decisions are made subjectively. When children are raised by members of the family other than their parents, it's called kinship care. Whether your grandchildren's parents are dead, or otherwise unable to bring them up, under the Children Act the court can make different types of 'order'. What follows is the picture, very broadly speaking, across the UK. It's essentially the same in England, Northern Ireland, Scotland and Wales, but there might be variations, so it's worth checking locally (See pages 262–3).

A residence order can be granted to enable your grandchildren to live with you until they're sixteen. If your grandchild has lived with you for three out of the past five years, you can apply for a special guardianship order. This is more secure than a residence order, because it doesn't end until the child is eighteen and can't be dissolved without the consent of the court. If you have either a residence order or a special guardianship order, then you *may* get financial assistance from your local authority, but it's entirely discretionary, and subject to a means test (see pages 265–6). Because these orders give you parental responsibility, some local authorities might use that as a reason not to pay you anything at all – the child is no longer 'in need', so as they see it, they no longer have any involvement. It's a good idea to talk to the local authority up front about what's available.

Fostering is another possibility for grandparents, but that's also complex. Local authorities normally select foster-parents and then train them, because the chances are that, over time, they're going to be fostering more than one child. They're always paid, and the amount is well established within bands which relate to how 'difficult' the child is considered to be. Payment can be quite substantial. The local authority retains parental responsibility for foster-children whoever fosters them. Grandparents who want to become foster-parents also have to be approved, and then they're entitled to be paid the same as other foster-parents. But they're not encouraged to foster – some cash-strapped local authorities seem to believe that grandparents should bring up their grandchildren for nothing, regardless of their financial situation.

In theory there are benefits – and sometimes local authority housing – available, but it's a big bone of contention. You might not be able to afford to give up your job in order to look after your grandchildren, but whether you're working or not, if you haven't much in the way of resources, taking on children can mean real financial hardship, and you should receive the help to which you're entitled.

There's another factor which can work against grandparents getting kinship care of their grandchildren. Local authorities are financially motivated to have children 'adopted out' – in other words to put them up for outside adoption. The reason for this is that in 2000, the government set a new target which aimed at increasing the number of adopted children by 5 per cent per annum, with a financial incentive for authorities who meet this target. The idea was to get children who are in care, out into families. This is obviously a good thing in itself. It's a fact that 25 per cent of people in prison have been in care, for example, and it's acknowledged that family life is a much better environment for children than an institution. Unfortunately, the target is arbitrarily and slavishly followed by some local authorities, even in the case of children for whom care needn't be an option – whose grandparents would take them. Rather than considering each case individually, they go for the 5 per cent. Apart from the government's bonus, there's the extra incentive that, once the child is adopted, it's deemed to be off their books both legally and financially – and knowing how strapped for resources local authorities are, all this may seem too good a plum to miss out on.

If your children wish, they can prevent any potential argument about custody in the eventuality of their death, by making a provision in their will that if they die you will automatically become your grandchildren's legal guardian(s). This will give you full parental responsibility. (They may also include some financial provision to help you raise the children.) It's a straightforward process to include this in a will. The last thing you'd want in the event of your child's death would be a dispute over their children, with the other grandparents, for example.

When You Want to Adopt

What if you want to adopt your grandchildren? Can you do this? When Enid and Bruno's son and daughter-in-law were killed on a climbing holiday, they adopted their two grandchildren. Bruno recalls: 'We didn't hesitate – we'd been involved in their lives from the moment they were born, we loved them and they loved us. It never occurred to us to do anything else. Their mother's parents are older than us, and not very fit, so they couldn't have done it, and the kids needed family. We got right on to social services and, thank goodness, they didn't object at all. The kids were spending the holiday with us when the accident happened, so they just stayed on. We changed their schools, and although it was a rough time for all of us, we know they're in the best place. It's been four years now, everything has settled down, and the children are really happy with us. Of course they'll always miss their mum and dad, but we're the next best thing.'

Bruno and Enid did the right thing in acting quickly. Whatever the circumstances surrounding your wish to adopt, you need to contact social services immediately and make your interest known. Make it clear to them that your grandchildren have been close to you all their lives and show how it would harm them to be separated from you. The Grandparents Association has a leaflet on arguments you can use to convince them (see page 262). If you delay you may find a court order has already been drawn up – they don't need your permission to do that – or even to let you know what's happening.

Bruno and Enid were lucky that the local authority was sympathetic. But in their case, there were no parents living. In general, social services and the courts discourage grandparents from adoption. First, because there's considered to be a likelihood of contact with the child's parents, which (rightly or wrongly) the court may not think desirable. Second, even if parental contact *is* approved, adoption by grandparents can be deemed inappropriate because it means you become the legal parents of your grandchild, and it therefore alters the lines of relationship in law – grandparents become parents, birth parents become the child's brother or sister, etc. It's not impossible for grandparents to adopt, but courts and social services tend to prefer other options – even adoption by strangers – so beware.

If you know your grandchildren are going to be put up for adoption and don't intend to take them on yourself, but want to maintain contact, talk to the local authority about getting an 'open adoption' (see pages 268–271). This means they will choose adoptive parents who are happy to maintain contact with you as the child's grandparents. If your grandchild is adopted by a couple who don't want to have any contact with you, then there's nothing you can do about it – you'll lose them completely. Then all that's left to you is to apply for permission to be put on your grandchild's contact register, so that when he/she is old enough, they'll be given your address and, if they wish, they can make contact with *you*.

Enid's grandson Justin isn't related to her by blood – he's adopted. 'When he was eleven, my son suddenly told Justin he was adopted. He didn't react to it very well. My son took him to see his birth grandmother, who he'd never met before. Justin came to see me afterwards, and said, "It makes me so sad you're not really my gran and that lady is. I didn't like her. I don't like thinking about it." Justin was confused and upset – and who can blame him? I feel sorry for his birth grandma, too – it's awful for her.' There's no way Justin's birth grandmother can make up the time she's lost, but there are things Enid could do to help. She could encourage Justin to find out more about her – maybe even contact her herself, and get to know her a little bit, then perhaps a relationship could be established.

It's tragic that birth grandparents can be divided from their grandchildren so comprehensively, but it's easy to see how it happens. A couple who adopt a child will want to make a fresh start, maybe they'll have parents of their own to fill the grandparent role, so the birth grandparents are surplus to requirements. That's not just hard on you, it's hard on the children, too. Their roots, their identity will be lost, and they have to cope with a whole new family without the back-up of someone loved and familiar.

All in all, the law is very complicated, and how it's interpreted varies both between local authorities, and from case to case (see pages 269–70). If you find yourself in any situation where taking on your grandchildren is on the cards, then it's essential to take legal advice. You might get help to pay for a solicitor, but you will be means tested and qualification will be subject to local authority criteria and rules.

Grandparents – A Wasted Resource?

Local authorities have a lot of freedom in how they place children and, on one level, it's obvious why. The law obliges them to act 'in the best interests of the child', but each case is different and has to be dealt with as such, so it's very far from straightforward. There are all kinds of considerations: in some cases, it's essential to get the children right away from their parent(s), so giving them to grandparents might make this difficult by putting the grandparents in the position of having to choose between their child and their grandchildren. But – and it's a big but – in general, there's a definite tendency for local authorities to undervalue grandparents as possible long-term carers, of whatever kind, for their grandchildren. There seems to be a distinct lack of imagination and sensitivity – a 'one size fits all' attitude to their reading of a situation and interpretation of the rules, and some are better at the job, and more empathetic, than others.

You'd think common sense would dictate that grandparents would be the first port of call, the obvious people to turn to, especially if they've had a long and close association with their grandchildren, something that's is absolutely vital when their world is turning upside down. Children *need* to be with someone they love, rather than strangers. What's more, grandparents will want to take all the siblings, where non-relatives might not, and surely that's a big consideration? What child would want to lose its brothers and sisters as well as its parents? In some cases, where it's appropriate, placing the children with their grandparents might make it easier for the whole family to get back on track and perhaps even function as a unit again. The fact is, where children can't be raised by their parents, and are in need, local authorities are supposed, as a *first resort*, to promote upbringing by members of the child's family (including, of course, grandparents). But some local authorities seem strangely suspicious of grandparents, and make them jump through hoops to prove the obvious – that children need to be loved.

It's not that social services are an evil entity – they're not a collective Cruella DeVille, intent on causing misery and pain. It's more that they don't think things through. And they're often afraid – afraid of going out on a limb, of making a mistake, of getting the blame for anything that might subsequently go wrong. It's always easier to say 'no' than 'yes'. But this fear can prevent them from doing their job properly. And the irony is they get pilloried anyway.

If you want to bring up your grandchildren, the best way, as always, is to talk to social services straight away and tell them you're up for it. Put yourself in the frame – don't wait for them to ask you – they might well not. You won't get any of the kinship care orders without a full assessment from them to evaluate the child's family situation from every angle. They won't necessarily get it right, but it's the place to start (see page 264).

There's also the matter of available resources and funding. In some cases lack of either might significantly affect their recommendations and decisions. It can appear as though they're looking for the cheapest, rather than the best solution. They have to make dramatic, sometimes instant decisions across county boundaries, and if you do gain custody, inter-necine wars can break out between different local authorities over who gives what support. This was Gail and Richie's experience, when they took over care of their two grand-children, aged six and eighteen months. Gail says:

> Our foster-daughter Gina was addicted to alcohol, and the children's lives were chaos. We sat down with social serv-ices and their other grandparents to make a 'care plan', and were given a family placement, with a view to being able to adopt later. It was left open-ended for a few months, because it was hoped that Gina might get her life back on track. Ritchie and I were still working, but I took four months' unpaid leave. Time went on and Gina didn't improve at all. We were worried about money – I had to go back to work, and so we put the baby in a nursery, but then social services suddenly told us that if we didn't agree to keep them, they'd both be put up for open adoption – which would mean, effectively, separating them from each other, as well as from us. They denied they'd ever made a care plan with us that would lead to us adopting. Of course we said we wanted them, and after they'd been with us for nine months, we

were given a residence order. We got a special guardianship order in 2006. Things aren't great from a money point of view. We have very little financial help, and no other kind of support at all for the children, who have both had terrific problems for a long time.

We have no faith in social services whatsoever now. Our experience has been that you have to fight for every little thing while they only worry about their budget. They batter you down, and it's very wearing. You just can't fight them *and* look after the children – it would make you ill.

It's a great pity Gail and Richie feel they've been deserted. Even if there isn't the cash to help them, they're entitled to back-up and support services – social services shouldn't merely hand the children over and walk away. It's in the local authority's interests, as well as the children's, to have their grandparents caring for them in a stable and loving environment. Sandra, who's bringing up her grandson Darren feels much the same. 'I've found social services completely useless. They just left me to it, so I've managed without them. But you're vulnerable. I do worry. What if they were suddenly to decide I'm too old, for example? Any change of circumstances now would be horrific for Darren.'

There's a big image issue here for social services in the UK, and it needs to be addressed. The local authorities who do a superb job – and there will be some – are being devalued by the ones who don't. Quite apart from all the unhappiness they cause, a hugely valuable resource – grandparents – can be left in a vacuum, as they struggle to fill a vital role that would otherwise cost local authorities time and money they can ill afford. It makes no sense.

Transforming Children's Lives

Whatever the situation causing grandparents to take over the parenting role – and it's always heart-rending – there's very clear evidence they can transform their grandchildren's lives, and bring something wonderful out of disaster or potential tragedy – well-adjusted young people equipped to take their place in society and have a happy, productive life.

Children who can't be brought up by their parents, because of death, drugs, abuse, or some other violent and/or horrifying circumstance, have suffered damage, and it can be far-reaching. But it's freely acknowledged that grandparents can counteract this much more successfully than any institution. And as far as adoption or fostering is concerned, in the aftermath of whatever catastrophe has torn their lives apart, grandparents can give them what strangers, however well-intentioned and loving, can never provide. It doesn't take rocket science to work out why – we're their roots, the solid base that keeps them grounded and secure. We share a history, and we love them. They can trust us with their lives – and they do.

But it can be a long and painstaking process, simply helping them to *be* children. Candice and Tony's daughter is a drug addict, and they took over the care of their two grandchildren, Natasha and Benjamin, when they were seven and two. Candice says:

> Our daughter was in and out of prison and the children had been living an appalling life – violence, neglect, abuse – they had massive problems. How could they not? Natasha had shoplifted to instructions; she'd smuggled drugs into prison in her mouth, when she visited her mum; she'd been hit by a drug dealer when she was four; her father used to hit her too . . . They'd moved house so often to escape the

police that she'd never learned to read or write. As she got a bit older she effectively became her mother's carer, and hid drugs from her.

Benjamin was really only a baby, but he'd learned things too – he'd hide food in his nappy because he didn't know when he was going to get any more. They were two miniature adults, self-centred, self-obsessed; they'd had to be, to survive. They'd had experiences no child should have. We put Benjamin in a nursery, and at first he was completely at a loss. He couldn't believe he had no responsibility, that all he had to do was play – he didn't know *how* to play.

After two years with us, they were getting better, but they still had a lot of problems. Benjamin was wetting the bed, and Natasha was having nightmares about men with knives. She was full of grief, and loss, and pain. We spent a lot of time teaching her to read. She's almost fourteen now. She still has anger management counselling, and she's in the bottom sets at school, although she's bright, and very beautiful – into make-up and boys. She's stolen money from us, and we read her the riot act sometimes. It's worrying, because she hides her real feelings, and she's a radar for kids like her. It's been easier for Benjamin, because he's had a normal upbringing with us since before he was two.

We have a residence order until they're sixteen. Tony and I inherited them and their background, and we try to mitigate it. I expect they'll make mistakes – everyone does – but they know we love them, and we work together. We dwell on the positive things, showing Natasha her family tree, and pointing out all the people on it who have made a success of their lives. We tell her she doesn't need to be like her parents. I worry that their mum and dad are loose cannons – their mum is in jail right now. We have to take the long-term view.

What Candice and Tony have done – and are still doing – is giving their grandchildren back their childhood. Some of the innocence which was lost can never be reclaimed, but they've gone a long way to put the past in its place, and to strengthen the children for the future. The most loving parent couldn't have done any more. They've saved them.

Natasha and Benjamin's parents are a continued presence in their lives and, as such, have to be taken into account. This is true for Sabina and Angus, who are bringing up their grandsons Robin and Greg. Sabina says:

In many ways we've been looking after them since they were babies, because our daughter Yvette has never given them a steady home. She was always a wild child – she ran away from home when she was fifteen. Yvette was made redundant when the boys were two years old and six months old – she had no social life and no cash, and got very depressed. I was still working full-time, and we saw the children every day. I offered to become a registered childminder, so I could look after her two, and make enough money to give up my job. Yvette didn't wait for me to get organised, though – she just went straight out and got a job on nightshift. I was working all day and then going to her place to look after Robin and Greg all night, so they moved in with us from Monday to Friday and went home at weekends – I almost had a breakdown because of all the work.

Then I got myself registered, and it all seemed to be going well. Yvette got tax credit and was paying me, but suddenly she stopped. She rang one day to say she wasn't getting any money any longer, because she hadn't paid her rent. It wasn't true, of course. Social services had found out she hadn't been working *at all* – she'd just been living on the child benefit herself – so they'd stopped it. With no money for rent, they didn't have anywhere to live, and they moved in with us. We set a few little rules for Yvette. We said, you can't act as though you're a single girl, but after a couple of weeks she went out and didn't come back. She just left the boys with us. Then, out of the blue, we got a solicitor's letter saying that we'd taken her children from her! We got ourselves a solicitor double quick, and applied for a residence order. The idea wasn't to cut her off – she'd be able to have them on Saturdays. They gave us an interim order for twelve weeks, so the kids could live with us while social services assessed us and did reports on us and Yvette.

Yvette was homeless – she was just staying with any friend who'd have her, really. She'd phone every week and tell us where to take the kids for the Saturday visit. On the seventh week she didn't ring, so we drove to the place we'd met her the week before and knocked on the door – they'd never even heard of her. Robin was very, very upset that his mum wasn't there.

When the time came for the court hearing, Yvette didn't show up, and her solicitor didn't know where she was, so we got the residence order by default. She disappeared for a year after that – we still don't know why.

It was a hard time for the boys: there was no contact; they didn't know where their mum had gone; they both developed problems. Robin would never go to bed. I slept outside his bedroom door for a whole year. It was exhausting. And he ate hardly anything. You can't wonder – he was so mixed up. On his fourth birthday, for example, Yvette sent him a card. He opened it and it said 'Love from Mummy'. He threw it away.

Then one day Yvette just phoned, and said would we like to meet our new granddaughter? Could she bring her round? I was too gobsmacked to be cross. She walked in with this four-month-old baby, as if she'd never been away, and talked to the boys as though the last year hadn't happened. Robin was reserved and, of course, Greg didn't know her, but they thawed a bit. She was living with the baby's dad so, gradually, I allowed them to spend a couple of hours with her now and then. I rationalised it to myself – after all, why would we stop them seeing her? As long as she wasn't harming them.

This has gone on for nine years. Now, we even let Yvette have them overnight sometimes. It's hard to do it, but as we see it, it's right. We've made sure that both boys understand they don't have to go – they only have to say no and it's OK. And if they want to come home at any point during the visit, they know we'll always fetch them. Occasionally Greg does refuse to go.

Yvette can't understand why I'm not the same with their sister as with the other two. But how could I be? I can't allow myself to get close to her for a lot of reasons. For one thing, I wouldn't want Robin and Greg to be jealous. They already wonder why their mum has got her and not them. And they do care about Yvette. We decided we'd like to move abroad, but we can't because the residence order specifies we have to live within a certain distance of their mother, but in any case, Robin wouldn't want to leave her. I find that hard – *we* made them who they are. But the choice must be theirs. As long as they're happy and safe, that's what we want for them.

They have a good life – all the normal stuff, like football, and so on, and we're proud of the way they've coped. They're well-adjusted. They don't call us Mum and Dad, but on Angus's birthday, Greg gave him a card. On the front it had 'Lots of love, Dad', but inside it said, 'I know you're not my dad, but this is because you *are*.'

Yvette's presence has got to be unsettling for Robin and Greg – she's their mother, but they don't live with her, like their half-sister does. Of course they ask themselves why. Children can blame themselves in situations like this – was it something *they* did? But Sabina and Angus have managed to strike a balance that allows the children to have regular contact with Yvette, yet feel secure, loved and wanted in their own world, with their grandparents. It's an amazing feat.

The Second Time Round

In rescuing their grandchildren, grandparents who become second-time-round parents risk losing *themselves* – plans and dreams they have for their later years are put on hold, perhaps for ever. Once again, life is lived in the present tense, as it was when they were raising their first family; once again, someone else's needs and wants have to come before their own; once again, the expense of raising children restricts their options. And this time they can't look forward thirty years to when they'll have all the leisure and freedom in the world – this time they might not have thirty years left.

However much they love their grandchildren, and however willingly they make the decision to raise them, there are going to be moments when they look at their life and wonder, wistfully, what it might have been like to be 'normal' grandparents. But probably not often; the family tragedies that have led them here will have transcended any wishful thinking. They sacrifice themselves without hesitation. It's love on a grand scale.

Anthea and Scott are bringing up their two granddaughters, who are five and three. Anthea says:

Sometimes we look round and think 'what have we done?' But then, what else *could* we have done – they're our family and we love them. The girls have had amazing problems in their lives, and it would have been very damaging for them to have been sent somewhere else. At fifty-three, I'm still fit and active, but it's physically hard for us. Scott is sixty. He'll be in his seventies when they're teenagers. He hasn't been able to retire because we can't afford for him to stop working. He has dropped one day a week, but we need to save for the future. If all this hadn't happened, we'd have a very different life. As it is, we can't go out without getting a babysitter. Rather than being ourselves, we're still the mum and dad partnership we always were. It's strange – my younger daughter has the grandma role – she's the one who takes them out for days, and for little sleepovers. She gets to spoil them – *I'm* the frazzled mum. But of course we don't regret it. We don't have the energy levels we had when we were young, but we do have more wisdom, I think. We'll always be here for them. We know they're safe, and the joy in their faces when they smile is worth everything.

This is a reversal of roles – Anthea and Scott have traded the joys of grandparenting for the rewards of parenting. Manny and Della have done the same. They've been caring for their eight-year-old granddaughter Billie since she was three. Della remarks, 'We've turned back the clock. It's funny to think we had *our* children young so we could have fun once they'd grown up – but no. I'm aware I'm a grandma, not a mum, but it's hard to remember sometimes. And I feel guilty about my other grandchildren – I just don't have the time to spend with them, like a grandma should, and as I'd like to do.'

For Martha bringing up her grandson hasn't just affected her, it's changed her daughter Sacha's life too. 'My grandson was only three when his mum died, and since he had no dad, he came to live with me. My younger daughter was at university at the time. She was marvellous – she knew I had enough problems. After she graduated she came home to live with me, and that was lovely for us both. I'm divorced, and although I've had relationships in the past few years, none has worked out – it's too much of a strain. I can't pretend it's easy bringing up a child at my age. Being a full-time parent again is hard work. I still look forward to having grandchildren when Sacha has children, then I can be a proper granny – you know, spoil them and give them back.'

It's a sad fact that raising your grandchildren deprives you of the simple pleasures of being a grandparent. It's a trade-off, and one these grandparents make without a second thought.

BEFORE YOU TAKE ON ANY KIND OF CHILDCARE

Talk to your partner – do you *really* want to do it?

Think it through carefully.

How fit are you – be honest?

What time do you have?

Do you need to work?

How far away do you live?

How much could you cope with?

Talk it through with your children.

Don't be afraid to say no – explain, gently, why.

If it's 'yes', make a plan – and agree it with your children.

It's reasonable to ask for expenses.

Agree details like food and discipline with your children.

CHILDMINDING: ISSUES TO DECIDE

Will you register formally?

Where will it take place – your home or theirs?

Will your home or garden need child-proofing?

Agree the hours – don't allow them to be *too* flexible.

Make sure there's back-up in place.

Agree on methods of discipline.

Agree on food strategies.

Plan what the children will be doing – agree it with their parents.

Talk about house cleaning expectations – you shouldn't be doing it.

6

Keeping the Closeness

The third millennium is the age of the extended family. As divorce and separation become increasingly common and marriage itself becomes rarer, the traditional, close-knit nuclear family is giving way to a very different concept – a loosely connected collection of fragments, strung together with no discernible centre. Families are extended in a geographical way, too, across the globe, as children grow up and move away from their roots, and parents retire and do the same. A lot of modern families fall into one – or even all – of these categories, and this has a significant effect on the way they function. That it doesn't necessarily prevent them from functioning altogether, is clear proof that the family is still an incredibly strong entity – alive, and well, and living in Scotland and Sri Lanka, St Austell and Australia, Huddersfield and Hong Kong.

But being part of any kind of extended family isn't easy. If your children live on the other side of the world, for example, then your grandchildren can't, however hard you all try, be a casual daily or weekly part of your life. Even if they only live across the Channel, or at the other end of the UK, they won't be popping in after school to show you their latest drawing. This doesn't mean you need to regard them as lost to you, or resign yourself to becoming comparative strangers – far from it – but the relationship will need working at.

If you or your children are divorced, remarried, or in a new relationship, then that will need work too because step-children, step-grandchildren, step-grandparents – a whole array of different people – can be daunting for everyone: confusing and difficult for young and old alike. But, carefully handled, all these ramifications can become an amazingly solid, loving unit. As grandparents, you can play a huge part in making this happen – in many ways, you're still the heart and soul of the family, and this puts you in a unique position to draw it together.

It won't always be possible (see Chapter 7), but it's worth the effort – think of all that love. There are ways to overcome the barriers of both emotional and physical distance. Yes, the chain can be so long and fine it's virtually invisible – but it's still there, to be picked up, polished and treasured.

Long-Distance Grandparents

Probably the thing grandparents want most is to see more of their grandchildren. The urge to connect with them is almost irresistible. It's as though, once our own children have grown up, we transfer some part of our most primeval protective and nurturing urges to the next generation. It's not just a wish, it's a need, and if we don't fulfil it we can feel deprived – even bereft.

But for some grandparents it's just a dream. Mervyn and Thelma feel like this. Their son Kerry and his family live in New Zealand. Mervyn describes their situation:

> Kerry moved to New Zealand twelve years ago and got married there. We went over for the wedding, and we've been for a couple of holidays, but gradually, they've become more distant with us. They sent us pictures of our two grandsons when they were born, and we still exchange letters and photos, but they don't seem to want to make the effort. His wife's parents live near them, and when we read what they've all been up to it nearly breaks our hearts. Oh, we don't grudge the other grandparents what they've got – but we do envy them, because we want it too. They haven't asked us over for about three years. They keep saying they're going to make a trip here, but it never happens. And we know they'll never come back to live. Those kids don't know us at all.

This is a tragedy for everyone: for Thelma and Mervyn, because they're missing out on the joy of knowing their grandsons; for the grandchildren themselves, who have lost a vital connection to their roots, and all the love that Mervyn and Thelma have to give them; and for Kerry, who's allowing his own parents to fade into the background of his life. It's not too late to repair this, but it will have to be Mervyn and Thelma who do so. Instead of worrying that they're not wanted and standing back, they could start acting as though they know they *are* wanted – that it's a foregone conclusion – and take the initiative: start phoning more frequently, email more often, perhaps plan a trip that includes New Zealand, and say they'll be coming to see everyone. They don't have to ask to be put up – they could stay in a hotel, or maybe hire a motor home.

And they *are* likely to be wanted and welcomed. Kerry would probably be thrilled to bits to see his parents. He's simply made the common mistake of letting habit get in the way. For the children, it would be an exciting event, something to look forward to. It would establish Mervyn and Thelma firmly in the minds of their grandsons, and maybe kick off a whole new level of communication. After all, what have they got to lose? If they leave this situation as it is, their grandchildren might never learn to love them.

The world is a big place, but it's a lot smaller than it was in our grandparents' day as Una and Theo know. Their daughter Dee lives with her husband, Aidan, and two daughters, Giselle and Roseanne, in Singapore, and the whole family works hard to stay emotionally close – and succeeds. Una explains:

They moved before the elder, Giselle, was two, and we hoped they might come back one day, but they've made their lives out there. It's where I was born, and some of my family is still there. I swapped cultures, too – I'm Singapore Chinese, and came to Britain when I was a young woman, and brought up my children without any of the background support you get from your close family, so I know what it's like for Dee.

I went out for a few weeks to help when Roseanne was born, but now we see them for a few weeks once a year. Naturally we wish it were more but, although we used to go once a year, we're not easily able to travel that far any

more, and our daughter and son-in-law work full-time, so they
come when they can. Giselle is twelve and Roseanne is nine, so
for the last three or four years they've visited us on their own.

We keep in touch a lot. Dee makes videos and sends
them, and we talk on the phone every other day or so. But
as they get older they're developing their own lives, and
don't chat for too long. They love us, and when they visit
us they're relaxed and comfortable but, each time, they have
to come to terms with the difference in the two cultures.
Those differences will broaden their experience, which will
be good for them, but for us it's hard. We've missed seeing
their progress: the milestones – school concerts – all the
little details. Our younger daughter has two girls, and they
live close by, so we make the most of them.

Una and Theo are lucky that they have grandchildren they
can see often, although, of course, it doesn't stop them missing
the others. Dee says, 'We need to stay here now until the
girls have finished school. It's a positive experience for them
– they're learning Chinese, and living in a different culture,
but we know it's not good for my parents – the journey is so
long – and it's very hot here for them. I ring Mum three or
four times a week on my way home from work, and we keep
up to date. You can make things happen if you've a mind to
do it. If the girls go to university in Britain, we may well
move back then, but we can't tell what's going to happen –
we're guests in this country, and the future isn't necessarily in
our hands.' Giselle says, 'We do miss Grandma and Granddad,
but we look forward to our holiday with them every year. I
suppose they have an image of us in their minds that's always
a little bit out of date, and they have to learn us all over again
when we go. We talk on the phone a lot, and when they
email me, I always email them back.'

Giselle and Roseanne's other grandparents, Alma and Jerome, are younger and fitter, and go to Singapore every year for a month. Alma describes her feelings: 'We were very upset we were missing those lovely early years, but now they're older we see them twice a year – they come to us for a week, and we go for an annual holiday in the Far East. We try to choose a time when they're on holiday too, so we can travel with them. We're doing it now, because we know we won't be fit indefinitely.'

As Dee says, everyone has to want to make things happen – and then they will. It's a big responsibility from the other side too, if you're an only child and your parents live thousands of miles away, especially if they aren't very well. Hanako is Japanese and she and her Iranian husband, Amir, live in the UK with their two children, Ethan and Maya, who are six and three. Hanako's parents still live in Japan.

Mum and Dad are in their seventies, and Dad couldn't travel here – it takes twenty-four hours – there's no way he could make the journey. And he's not well enough for Mum to leave him to visit us. So the only way they get to see the children is if we take them to Japan, and we can't do that very often.

It's been particularly tough for them both because the Japanese custom is for a daughter to go back to live with her parents for the first three months of a baby's life. She just rests, and the family look after her. Sounds good, doesn't it? It's so much taken for granted as a tradition in Japan, and there's a lot to be said for everyone being close together. But that's been impossible.

I took both children for an eight-week stay when they were six months old. It isn't the same, but it's the best we could do. Amir couldn't leave work for so long, but he came out for the last fortnight to pick us up. It was fantastic for Mum and Dad, but very, very hard on Amir to miss two months of Ethan's life – they change so much at that age. Still, what could we do? Mum and Dad wouldn't have seen them as babies, otherwise.

Now we try to take them every year, but it's expensive, and to go all that way you need to stay a while, so Ethan's seen them four times, and Maya only twice. Of course, we keep in touch – Dad has a computer and digital camera and he did a movie, complete with titles and music – it was beautiful. It's given him a new hobby! And they send a box every month, with toys, sweets, and Japanese children's books. We have chats on the speaker phone, and by email, and my parents make an effort with English, but they don't speak it fluently. Ethan's learning Japanese, and last time we came home, he couldn't speak English! It took him about ten days to get back to normal.

Amir says: 'It's hard on Hanako's parents – but it's hard on the kids, too – it's an important relationship and they're all missing out. It's a good thing my mum and dad are in Britain, and they can see them often. We never dump them though, because Mum runs her own business and she's really busy. But she's very hands-on – it's the Iranian way for families to be close.'

Amir's right – children need the grandparent connection as much as grandparents themselves, but they probably won't realise what they're missing. Sending family packages and emails is very worthwhile, especially if they're sent direct to the children themselves. Youngsters love opening letters and parcels. They'd look forward to the post if there was a chance of something for *them*. It doesn't have to be a gift – just a small note or a card, or a photo of you – anything, really.

Clover and Warren and their children all live in the UK, but a very long way apart, and so have to depend on the phone for their most frequent contact. Clover says, 'It's hard for small children to hold a telephone conversation. They'll say, "I don't want to talk to you any more now." I hear them at the other end of the line, and I want to be with them all. I'm a teacher, and I spend more time with other people's children than my own grandchildren.'

The very young do find it hard to fathom a phone – the silences, the emergence from nowhere of familiar voices; the concept of questions and answers; the detachment of it all. Mother of three Gillian says, 'My youngest daughter is two, and an absolute scream on the phone. She likes it, but hasn't quite got the idea yet. She was chatting with my father-in-law, when he sneezed, and she tried to pass him a tissue down the phone!'

It isn't only the very young who struggle, older children can easily get bored too: 'Hi, Grandpa . . . Bye, Grandpa!' It's a chore for children to have to answer questions about what they've been doing, what they had for dinner – they'd prefer you to tell them what *you've* been doing – children are creatures of action and reaction. But cutting you off abruptly doesn't mean they don't care about you; in a way it's a sign of security. It means they know you're there, a reliable, constant part of their lives. They're not worried you're going to disappear – you're real to them. In other words, you've cracked it.

Making It Work

If distance is a fact in your family life, try to work out a system, and set a precedent. What might seem a big deal to begin with will quickly become the norm, an established thing. Roz and Bill have three daughters and, while they only live an hour and a half's drive from Roz's parents, Bill's parents, Vanessa and Murray, who are retired, live in France. Roz told us:

> Obviously it would be more convenient for all of us if they were on the doorstep, but I think, in some ways, this works better. We get to have my mum and dad to stay for weekends and, because they're not working, Bill's mum and dad will come to stay during the week sometimes when we really, really need babysitting. That way they don't all feel too much like doormats. We're very conscious that they've got their own lives – we don't expect them to be at our beck and call – they're busy people. But it's not just about helping us, the kids really appreciate it. It *is* more of a special thing. It's more fun; a closer relationship. If they saw their grandparents every day it would be very mundane. They stay with both sets on their own for weekends or the odd week in the school holidays. They love it, our parents love it – and Bill and I get the girls out of our hair for a few days or the chance to go away on our own.
>
> We get on well with both sets, and so having them to stay, or going to stay with them, is something we're very happy to do often. We have super weekends at my parents' house, and great holidays in France with Vanessa and Murray. And we're not big on lots of organised activities for the kids at weekends, like football or dance classes, specifically because it would make it harder for us do that. I suppose we are conscious of making sure that we see everyone, but it isn't hard to do – I think, I hope, everybody benefits.

Bill's mother, Vanessa says:

> Roz and Bill make sure we see a lot of the children. We don't feel cut off at all – they're really good about it, very

fair. When the children were born, Roz's mum went to stay for the first week, and then we were invited for a few days straight after that. We never feel we're missing out. Perhaps their other grandparents might see them a bit more often than we do, but we tend to get them for much longer every time – a week or even two – which means they chat to us in more detail about their lives. We're exhausted when they leave, but it's wonderful. You forget yourself, and just be with them. And unlike Roz's parents, we don't work now, so we can come and visit the children at home for longer, pick them up from school, meet their friends and so on. In-between we phone a lot, and we see each other on the computer camera, although I'm not as keen on that.

It's true that Vanessa and Murray are lucky. But the whole family wants to make it work.

Hywell and Gwen aren't so fortunate with their daughter Wendy and son-in-law Julian. Gwen explains:

Our grandson is five now, and sees much more of Julian's family than us. We live a couple of hundred miles away, but it's not that bad a journey. You'd think it was Timbuktu the way they um and ah about visiting us. It takes three or four hours, but it's an easy drive. They always seem to have something else on – often with his parents, who live about an hour away. Somehow they manage to find the time to see *them*. I can't pretend we're not hurt, and a bit jealous, when we hear our grandson talking about where he's been with his other grandparents, and what they've done. *We* could do all that with him, too. We feel so out of touch. I mean, we're not even sure what kind of presents to buy him because we don't know exactly what stage he's in at any given time. Of course, now he's started school, he's in a whole different world. Perhaps it sounds self-pitying, but we wonder what we've done to deserve this. Don't they like us as much as the others?

This is a classic moment for a family chat. Hywell and Gwen are on the brink of a disaster here. If they sit brooding about what's happening, instead of getting it out in the open, either they'll just drift further out of their grandson's life, or it will suddenly come to a head and end in an argument that could blow the family apart. It's possible that Wendy and Julian have no idea how they feel, and that a chat could make all the difference. They do live further away, but Wendy and Julian could visit occasionally. And if travelling two hundred miles doesn't appeal, Hywell and Gwen could invite themselves to stay now and again. Of course, it's possible they *do* prefer to be with Julian's parents. If that's the case, then it's even more important for Hywell and Gwen to point out all they're missing. But it's vital for them to talk calmly, without accusing their children of not caring, or of having favourites. That would just make Wendy and Julian defensive – and angry. If they explain how they feel, say it makes them sad, things could change for the better. They haven't fallen out, there's no row to get over and, if they handle things tactfully, there needn't be. The important thing is to break this pattern by taking active steps rather than dwelling on how bad it all is.

Contact doesn't need to take the form of extended stays or bed-and-breakfast. Amelia and Sean live a fair way from Sean's parents, who are both still working. Amelia says, 'We know they can't come to us very often – so we just go there. Instead of planning a big weekend and having Sean's mum cook herself to a standstill, we'll say we're going to be passing, we'll come and eat with you – shall we collect some fish and chips to bring in? Of course she usually says not to bother, that she'll cook us a meal, but she knows she doesn't have to, that we're trying not to put on her.' Taking the initiative in this way is safe and undemanding for Sean's parents. Exactly how you go about getting together will depend on your relationship with your children.

Special Measures

Sometimes the only way to make sure you see your grandchildren is to have a major event. Even if it's only once a year, it's better than nothing. Maeve and Trevor do this. Maeve describes what they do:

We live a very long way from all our children, meeting up is expensive and difficult for all of us. Trevor has just retired but I'm still working, and that makes it even harder. As a result, we only see our grandchildren two or three times a year. They're very young – five, four, three and two, and although we phone quite often, it's not the same. They always know we're there, and our children talk about us a lot, but it can't replace actually seeing them. I think about them so much. And distance affects them. When we first see them they're reluctant and shy, and it takes time for them to come round.

We've just built a small holiday house on a lake, and this year, for the first time, we had all our children and grandchildren to stay at the same time for three weeks of the summer break. It was a crowd, but we were so happy! It took the children about ten days to relax, and then something happened – they seemed to find another kind of confidence for the first time. Trevor and our eldest granddaughter shared a small secret together, which was lovely to watch. And when our youngest was upset, he came to me – he wanted my protection. What a wonderful feeling! Other grandparents might take that for granted, but we've never really had anything like it before. I just sit and watch them – drink them in.

I know when they're older I'll be retired and have the time to spend with them. They can come and stay with us then, but they have to get to know us first. It will be OK; they'll catch up. I'm living for that time.

Maeve and Trevor's children are doing the right thing by talking about them to their grandchildren. Telling stories, and looking at photographs is a good way to keep them alive in young children's minds and imagination.

Maeve and Trevor decided not to let circumstances dictate to them. By building a house where they can all get together, they've made something good happen. But, of course, it needn't mean a major building programme. Vernon and Stacey rent a cottage for a week in the summer holidays every year, and all their seven grandchildren come to stay without their parents. Vernon explains: 'We call it our activity week and it's quite regimented, like a camp. I draw up a list of things we're going to do, and there are "orders for the day". We'll take on projects like making boats and launching them. One year we made puppets – we still have them. We go ice-skating, sleep in tents, cook outside – it's a real outdoorsy thing.' Stacey adds: 'One year we were sleeping in a field and my grandson said, "Are you hating this, Granny?" I wasn't, because I was with them all. It's very important to do things like that together. They'll remember it.'

What Vernon and Stacey are doing is called 'team-building' when it happens within companies, and it's regarded as a valuable part of working life. To do it with your grandchildren in this way cements the family unit. It's great for cousins to get to know one another so well; it can forge friendships that last a lifetime. All that's needed is a plan and the confidence to carry it out. Tina's parents, Wally and Violet, live three hundred miles away. Her daughters are six and four.

It's especially hard on Mum. They do visit us quite regularly though. They have a caravan and they come down in it and stay a few nights to look after the children for us. The girls have seen Gran and Granddad more often in their caravan than in their house, and I wonder if they think Mum and Dad live in it all the time! They always take it to France and Spain for the summer, and I've suggested they have the girls along, but Mum won't do it. She says it's not convenient. I think it would be perfect and I've tried to tell her how much they'd all enjoy it – and they'd have the freedom of the kids without us breathing over their shoulders. But not so far. I think she feels guilty about it – but not guilty enough! I daresay they will take them soon, now they're getting a little bit older. They're missing out on the children – and I miss *them*, too. I wish they lived as near as my husband's parents, who are only five miles away.

It is probably anxiety that's preventing Violet and Wally from taking their granddaughters away with them. Young children are a big responsibility – in fact, older ones are too, as Magnus and Colleen found when they gave their two granddaughters a very special treat.

Carys and Stella are twelve and fourteen. They live in New Zealand, and we only see them once a year, so last year we decided to make it spectacular. We like going on cruises, and we'd said that when they were older we'd take them with us. They kept on asking when it would be, so we said – OK, we'll do it now, while we're still fit enough, and booked a five-day cruise on the *Queen Mary* for the four of us. They flew over on their own and we took them to the ship. When they saw the size of it, the first thing they said was, 'Will it sink?' Their favourite movie is *Titanic!*

The girls had a wonderful time, but we were very strict with them about bedtimes and things like that. They were very good, but we did have one drama. They were supposed to meet us at a certain time for dinner, and they didn't turn up – no Carys, no Stella. Vernon searched the ship from end to end. He was getting annoyed, and I was too. He found them and brought them back and I blew up. I told them how worried I'd been, and made them promise not to do it again. I'd had visions of phoning their parents and telling them the girls had gone overboard!

This trip was an expensive, once-in-a-lifetime thing to do, but it doesn't need to be so elaborate. Anything you plan to do with your grandchildren will be appreciated by them, whether it's a few days under canvas or a day trip to a theme park or zoo. It's being with *you* that counts.

For Lois and Dominic, the odd weekend, or even week, wouldn't be enough. When they retired they moved hundreds of miles, specifically to be near their children. Dominic says:

Lois and I were born in the far north of Scotland and we'd always lived there, but our three children all ended up in London, married to people from the south. They settled there, and didn't have plans to come back north. Our eldest son asked us to move to live nearer them, and we wanted to, but at the time we had to say no, because Lois's mum was ill. Then, when I retired, we decided to go south for good. We didn't move onto their doorstep, we chose somewhere that was easy for them all to get to. We had no connections with the place, and it was a big wrench to leave Scotland but, as we see it, it's incumbent upon parents to move nearer to their families so they aren't a burden later. If you're going to move anyway – and a lot of people do when they retire – why not make it near to the people you love instead of among strangers?

We took the initiative, but then, over a period of time, our children moved to be still closer to *us* – now two live in the same village, and the third is about six miles away. With thirteen grandchildren, we're a clan! Our children realised that as their kids arrived we'd be a support system – for babysitting and everything else. We all thought it would be *fun* – and it is. Being a grandparent is a golden age. We've always been very close, had this huge family ethos, and our children wanted it for their children.

Lois agrees:

It *is* fun. We see our grandchildren all the time because we live round the corner – we're their second home. They stay overnight as and when. We had a swimming pool built and in the summer they're here every day. The older ones cook on a fire (with a bucket of water handy), and we enjoy it all immensely. It's as though we're at the centre of this spider's web, but I'm not the spider – it's me and all of their mums. Dominic and I don't act as a conduit, they have to tell each other things. That way it will all carry on when we're gone. We're very close to our children. We're home from home for all of them, and that's good, but we never drop in on *them* unannounced – we always telephone first. We treat them with respect – like people, not just appendages of ourselves. We think it's terribly, terribly important for parents to observe the same formalities and courtesies you would with friends.

It's true we do an awful lot with and for the children – we're here to provide services as needed, to step into the breach. All their parents work; they're very busy, and it can be hard. We can help with all that. It's a network and we all help each other. It's very rewarding – we have a ball.

Lois and Dominic are reaping the benefits of being so involved with their grandchildren – and their children like it too. Their son Barry says:

I think Mum and Dad realised we all wanted children and they had a choice: they could see us all from time to time in Scotland, or move here to be with us. They were making themselves available. They realise how lonely it can be coping with young children and full-time jobs when you're isolated from your family.

They have a large garden, and very cleverly built the swimming pool, which of course is a big draw. It's worked out wonderfully well. They see the kids, warts and all, rather than just on special occasions, and we're all together for birthdays and so on. They don't seem to take holidays, though I do wonder if Dad would be more inclined if Mum was up for it. She wants to be here – to give us somewhere to go when the children are ill, for example. They ought to have a break sometimes. But there you are – they love it as it is.

Lois and Dominic are part of a 1990s phenomenon called 'clustering', when it became the trend for families to move close together to provide mutual support. It can make sense, and work out well for everyone. But even with an enormous amount of emotional commitment, it can be difficult to bring off – people's financial and economic situations might make it impossible. Still, if you want to think of doing something like this, talk it through as a family – you might be surprised at the result.

Grandparents and Step-Families

Being part of a step-family, whatever your role, is a challenge as family dynamics shift and people try to adjust to new circumstances. For children, it can be particularly unsettling. Whatever age they are, they're quick to pick up on adult tensions and feelings. Children can worry when they sense the adults in their lives are struggling to come to terms with something new.

Making Them Feel Secure

Grandparents play an important role in making children feel secure and comfortable (see Chapter 7 and pages 269–271). In fact, your grandchildren will need you more than they've ever done; you play a crucial part in keeping their world on an even keel, even if it's you who's brought the 'stranger' into their lives.

Victor and Netta were both widowed when they married; Victor has four granddaughters. He says: 'All the girls were very close to my late wife, Adele, especially the eldest, and I was a bit worried they might resent Netta. We were careful, but they've been fine – relaxed and natural.' Netta remembers how she felt: 'I must admit I was a bit concerned, too, because I knew they all worshipped Victor. I didn't want them to think I was coming between them, or trying to take Adele's place. They welcomed me right from the start

– they're very nicely brought up children. But it's more than that – it's genuine, and we've become close. I'm more hands-on than I ever expected to be. When Victor and I told the girls we were going to get married, they immediately said, "Can we be bridesmaids?" None of them had ever done it before, so it was a big thrill for them. I remember at the wedding rehearsal, they started walking in front of me – that's where they thought they had to be!' Victor recalls: 'When they practised walking behind Netta, they didn't know how fast to go and were goose-stepping to keep up. They thought that's what you had to do – it was very funny.' Victor and Netta were conscious of the fact that they needed to tread carefully, and, as a result, no feelings have been hurt. The children didn't feel displaced because they knew Victor loved them. But they were right to take the possibility seriously. It's risky to assume that children will welcome a new family member straight away. After all, why should they? If they've lost a much-loved grandparent, then they're very likely to feel at least a little anxiety they're going to lose the other one, too.

Ted and Vicky discovered this when Ted's mother, Miriam, remarried after being divorced. Ted says:

Our two boys, Matt and Fabian, were five and seven when Mum and Dad split up. They love my dad, and we didn't lose touch, but he moved away so we don't get to see him so often. Then Mum started seeing Clem, and at first the kids didn't like him at all, although he's a lovely bloke. He's funny, with a big laugh, but it didn't matter what he did, the boys, Matt particularly, just ignored him. When Mum told us they were getting married, they were upset. They kept saying, 'Why does she have to?' They didn't want to go to the wedding; said they didn't care. You know how boys can be.

In the end, Mum had them round for tea and told them

she loved Clem, but it didn't mean she didn't love them just as much as ever. She said that grown-ups sometimes get lonely and that's how she was, now Granddad was living a long way away, and it would be nice for her to have someone to live with all the time, especially someone like Clem who made her laugh. Mum was great – she asked them how they'd feel if they were her. The boys were a bit grudging, but they came round eventually, and they all get on well now.

Probably what swung it for Miriam was the fact that she kept emphasising how much she still loved them – that they were still going to have her – and Clem too. She knew they were thinking Clem would take away the love that should be coming to *them*. Miriam talked to them and explained things in a way they could understand and relate to. She didn't just brush aside their worries – she took them seriously. She asked them how *they'd* feel. If you introduce an idea to a child, they can put themselves in someone else's place.

It's important, too, to give them time to get used to the new person, and learn to like them for themselves. In fact, left to itself, the problem might go away of its own accord, but you do need to keep an eye on it and take some action if it doesn't.

It's not only children who need time to adjust – sometimes it's the grandparents themselves. Vince has three boys under ten. He divorced their mother and his second wife, Stella, has three-year-old twins of her own. Vince's father, Bert, couldn't get on with them at all.

Dad had been fond of my first wife. They'd hit it off from the start, and he was very upset when we split. He was great with the kids, and really helped them cope with it all, but when he realised Stella and I were getting serious, he started staying away. He couldn't seem to handle seeing her in the house with my three.

The kids were really missing him – they couldn't understand what was going on – they kept asking me where their granddad was. Then, when we got married, he was always off-hand with Stella's twins. They're lovely little girls and they needed a granddad, too, but he more or less ignored them. Stella was upset, of course she was. In the end I said to Dad that we were a family, that all the kids were mine and Stella's together now, and he was their granddad, whether he liked it or not, so he should be fair and treat them all the same. Dad admitted that he hadn't wanted what he called 'outsiders', and said he wouldn't be able to love the twins as much as my lot. Well, I told him he'd have to learn, because we wanted him in our lives, and the kids needed him. I said if he wasn't careful he'd lose my boys too, because they love their little step-sisters. It's worked itself out, although it took a little while. To see Dad with the girls now, you'd think he was their real granddad – and as far as they're concerned, he is.

Vince did the right thing in talking to his father, and pointing out the facts: that the new family was there to stay. It was good too, that he warned him how easy it would be to lose his grandsons. It wasn't a threat, it was a clear-sighted look at what was happening. He knew his father was struggling with unfamiliar feelings, and didn't mean to be resentful. He wanted Bert to give them a chance. In that instance, Bert didn't put his grandchildren off their new step-mum, but he might have done. You can do a lot to calm any hostility or insecurity your grandchildren may be feeling about their step-parent, simply by being welcoming yourself.

The Green-Eyed Monster

Jealousy is all too likely to crop up in step-families; it's completely understandable. After all, the family structure is being altered in a fundamental way, and no one wants to be left out in the cold. Katrina and Giles were surprised to find themselves feeling like this when their daughter Marion remarried. Katrina recalls:

We like Seb, Marion's new husband, he's lovely, and we were pleased for Marion that our two grandsons took to him from the start. What we hadn't expected was how they took to Seb's mum and dad as well. They adore them – you can see it. They're a lot younger and fitter than us, and can do more things with them: they go off on cycling holidays, and we aren't fit enough to bike. Seb's dad is mad keen on football, and he takes the boys to the local club, where he's a member, so that's a lot of Saturdays out of the picture for us. They used to come round for the afternoon, but now they're at the match. I think they find us boring. The boys are seven and nine, and they used to like 'helping' Giles make model planes and ships and dinosaurs, but they're not interested now – it's all action.

If Katrina and Giles continue to stand on the sidelines, then their grandsons *will* move on without them. Some flexibility is called for here. For a start, perhaps they could learn to like football! Then they could go along with the others to matches and take everyone back to their house for tea afterwards. In any case, the football season doesn't last all year, so Katrina and Giles could make more of the summer months. There are plenty of things they could do in the fine weather. If Giles likes making models, he could build some remote-controlled boats or planes, and they'd all have fun with these, without having to be too strenuous about it. Or they could fly kites, or try fishing – another fairly gentle pastime. Why not ask the boys what *they'd* like to do – who knows what they might say? Developing new interests together would benefit them all. In any case, children's tastes change as they grow older (see Chapter 8), and it's a good thing for grandparents to keep up with them, even in a limited way.

When it's the children who are jealous in a step-family things can get trickier because they aren't necessarily going to respond to common sense or persuasion. Possessive instincts are part of their survival technique, they're programmed in, hard-wired. Merle and Steve found this when Merle's father, Conor, remarried. Merle says:

Our son and daughter are both under five and they worship Dad. He can do no wrong. They used to see him nearly every day and he'd be down on the floor with them, acting the fool. He was their slave. They've never had a granny, because Mum died a few years before they were born, and Steve's mum and dad have been dead for a decade, so Dad's their only grandparent – everything, really.

We were thrilled when he started seeing Marina. After all, he's only sixty-two – why not? And she's super. The kids got on well with her as granddad's 'friend'. We thought – how great for us all. But when she moved in with him it was a different story. The kids played her up, answered back. They were so naughty. They ran rings round Dad, too. It was mayhem. He couldn't understand it – they'd always eaten out of his hand – he'd never even had to raise his voice to them. They were running riot, so we decided not to visit so much. We thought if they missed him a bit they'd change. Dad wasn't happy about it – in fact, he still isn't. We haven't got back onto the old footing yet, and don't know if we can, until the children are older. Dad and Marina come round when they're in bed. They haven't fallen out with us, but Dad's broken up about it.

Keeping the children from their granddad now is the last thing they should be doing. They're behaving like this precisely *because* they're worried that Marina's presence might separate them from him – and their worst fears are coming true. All of them need to act quickly or several things might happen. The children might be missing their granddad now, but they're very young, and it won't take long for them to disconnect with him. Then just think what they'll miss out on. Another worry is that it might damage the relationship between Conor and Marina, and that would be a tragedy, too. Conor's missing his grandchildren, and it's a short step from there to blaming Marina for the situation. He won't necessarily mean to, but resentment might grow, with drastic consequences.

Once again, it needs a family chat. If all four adults get together and talk about what's happening, they can come to an agreement about the best way forward. Obviously, no one's interests are being served by cutting the children off from their grandfather. Merle and Steve could emphasise how much they'd like everything to get back on track, which would make Conor feel better, and Marina would have the chance to show how much she's prepared to try. After a chat like this, Conor could have a little talk with his grandchildren and explain to them that he loves them just as much, and that Marina will love them like he does. He could take the opportunity to tell them they're not being naughty, that he understands. They could arrange some outings together – to the seaside, the cinema, or even just the local playground. With some other attraction on offer, the children and Marina won't be in each other's faces, and the ice could be broken if they're all having fun. If these outings become a regular feature of their lives, they could gradually come to feel less jealous, stop punishing their grandfather, and accept Marina. Once again, time is a vital factor. They're under five years old and, at that age, the world is a very small place.

Reaping Some Benefits

Step-families needn't be all about angst. In some cases they can actually make things better. A new partner can repair the dent in *your* confidence. Bobby's granddaughters are seven and five. He lost his wife before they were born. His daughter Chelsie says, 'Bobby wasn't very comfortable with either of the girls. It's as though, without Mum, he couldn't get his head round babies and youngsters. My sister's kids are older, and he's close to them, but Mum was alive when they were little. He has a new partner now. She's got grandchildren of her own and she's helped him a lot. The girls don't call her Grandma, but they treat her as if she was their gran, and she's really lovely – she'll drop everything and help.' On his own, Bobby didn't feel properly equipped to take babies and toddlers on board and stood back. There's a generally held feeling that grandmothers and small babies go together, and that grandfathers come into play when the children grow a little older. Bobby's new wife has bolstered his confidence, not just because she's a nice person who loves children but because she's a woman which, in his mind, was the missing factor.

It isn't necessarily true, of course, and often the only reason it happens is because grandfathers think it's the norm and allow it. But it's risky. If you don't engage with your grandchildren, they don't engage with you, and the longer you leave it the harder it becomes to forge those bonds. The roundabout doesn't stop; the faster it goes, the more difficult it can be to jump on. That's not to say that if you don't imprint yourself when they're babies you've lost your grandchildren, just that, if you let them get too much of a head start, you have to overcome their shyness and unfamiliarity before you can reach them. Why make it more difficult for yourself? If you have no partner, whatever sex you are, get in there and love 'em – that's all they want – you don't need 'skills'.

When remarriage occurs before the birth of grandchildren, things can be much easier because they've never known or loved anyone else – but they'll still ask questions. Edgar and Marigold have been married for eighteen years. They were both widowed, and Marigold has one daughter and two grandchildren, aged eleven and eight. Marigold says, 'We've never sat them down and talked about it specifically, but they've gradually worked it out, and they said to my daughter, "Gramps isn't really your daddy, is he?" Not that it bothers them at all. They regard him as their granddad – and he is.' Edgar, who has no children of his own says, 'It's an easy way of doing it! I have a ready-made family. I was careful when they were born – I kept a bit of distance, because I didn't want to get in the way – there's another granddad. I didn't want to push, but if they had a use for me, then that was fine. I didn't expect it to happen, but to my surprise, it did. It's a different feeling, having grandchildren when you have no children. I had no real grandparents myself, so I didn't know how to *be* with them, but it's sorted itself out. I'm godfather to the eldest, too, and it's nice.' As Edgar has found, young children have an infinite amount of love to give – and all they need is for you to be there to accept it.

KEEPING UP COMMUNICATION

Don't	**Do**
Be passive.	Keep talking.
Assume they don't want to see you.	Look for ways to meet.
Dwell on the drawbacks.	Take the initiative – come up with suggestions.
Let it fester.	Have confidence – assume they want you.
Indulge in self-pity or jealousy.	Keep in touch – and send the *children* letters of their own.

IF YOU'VE DRIFTED APART

Don't
Settle for separation.
Have a row about it.
Accuse them of not caring.

Do
Talk to them.
Explain how you feel – without anger or resentment.
Listen to how they feel.

(contd.)

> Be prepared to meet them halfway.
> Make a plan together.
> Build up contact gradually.
> Write, phone, email.

STEP-FAMILIES – HOW THE CHILDREN MIGHT FEEL

Confused at this change in their world.

Insecure – what else might happen? What might it mean for *them*?

Jealous – do they have to share *their* people with this stranger?

Resentment at the stranger's presence – why don't they go away?

Hostile – '*I'm* not going to make friends with this person.'

HOW GRANDPARENTS CAN HELP

Be there for your grandchildren.

Listen to their worries – spend time with them.

Take those worries seriously.

Don't judge them – be understanding.

Talk to them, reassure them, explain what's happening and why it's no threat.

Let them know you'll always be there for them to confide in.

Tell them you love them; that their parent(s) love them.

If the new person is a step-parent, be welcoming yourself – set an example.

If it's your new partner, make sure you work together to include the children.

7

When Families Split Up

Britain has the highest divorce rate in Europe. Doom and gloom merchants regularly claim that marriage is dead, the family a moribund institution and that no one seems to care. Spouting on this state of affairs is the modern equivalent of saying 'the country's going to the dogs'. It's repeated so often it's become accepted as the norm. We hear of yet another divorce, shrug our shoulders and sigh philosophically at the inevitability of it, as though, like death and taxes, it's a part of daily life we can do nothing about: unpleasant, but unalterable.

While divorce statistics can't be denied, the rest is far from true – marriage is still what most couples aspire to, and families *do* survive the effects of a break-up, often against incredible odds. For the ones that don't, the cost in misery can be enormous. Divorce might have become an everyday thing, but there's nothing everyday about the emotions it generates – no tsunami could leave behind more devastation.

Couples struggle to come to terms with falling out of love: the resentments, jealousies and insecurities; the anger and pain; the bitterness and acrimony that can bubble under the surface of even the most 'civilised' separation. The children, whatever their age, are left clinging for dear life to the wreckage like little castaways, feeling afraid, anxious, even guilty, as though all of this is somehow their fault. Their parents might be doing everything they can to protect them from the worst of the fallout but, then again, they might not. Lost in their own unhappiness, some couples aren't strong enough to resist the urge for revenge: they take whatever tools are at hand to wreak it, and that can include their children – your grandchildren.

So where do you stand in all this? Watching your child's marriage collapse is bad enough. It can be hard, sometimes impossible, to steer a middle road and avoid taking sides, to be there for your own offspring, yet not dabble and make things worse. When you're a grandparent as well, you can be torn several ways at once. Your children need you, but so do your grandchildren. You're their rock in the midst of all the chaos as their world disintegrates around them. You're someone they can trust, someone familiar who isn't leaving them; a part of their lives that isn't changing. You're essential to their well-being and peace of mind.

Except, of course, that you *might* be leaving them – you might not have any say in the matter because for some couples you're a tool, too – a nice, handy, sharp one, excellent for drawing blood and causing pain in all kinds of ways. The fact that this will also almost certainly hurt their children might be overlooked in the heat of the battle to score points, and their desire to give rein to all that anger and insecurity. There may not be anything you can do about it without going to court (maybe not even then), because grandparents have absolutely no automatic legal right of access to their grandchildren. You can be left on the sidelines, watching in agony, helpless to intervene. Of course, it isn't always as bad as that; many separated couples recognise grandparents for what they are and can be – a force for good in an unstable situation. They won't cut you out, or hesitate to call on you.

But not all family splits arise out of divorce. Disagreements, even trivial ones, can become rows, people take sides, things are said, and suddenly the row is a feud, and people who, at bottom, love each other, can end up as strangers – sometimes for years, maybe for ever. This is tragic for everyone, and the fall out can separate you from your grandchildren.

So, if your child's relationship with their spouse or their relationship with you falls apart, how do you handle it? Do you draw your skirts away from the muddy overspill, or wade right in without your boots? There are as many answers to this question as there are families in trouble, and most of them will fall somewhere in the middle of those two extremes. There's no foolproof, fast solution, and there are no guarantees, but there *are* ways you can help to make things better for your grandchildren – and yourself.

Walking the Tightrope

One of the reasons why families fall apart, whether it's a couple who are splitting up, or a fracture across the generations, is that people don't talk to each other enough. They don't come out with what's bothering them while it's still a minor issue which could easily be fixed. Instead, they hold it in until they can't do so any longer, and it bursts out like a forest fire, destroying everything in its path. Small niggles can fester until they're huge resentments. And by this time, like all long-running wars, regrettable things will have been done or said by both sides, so who started it will have ceased to matter – everyone is culpable.

Keeping Your Balance

When your child's relationship falls apart you're bound to have an opinion about it – how could you not? You'll probably have been watching the situation deteriorate; you may have been drawn into it by the couple themselves, or even be considered to be part of the problem.

It's painful to see your child suffering, whether they're wronged, or in the wrong. A parent's instinct is to try to make everything all right again. But this is one instance where that's unlikely, if not impossible. Not only can't you make it go away, you can't risk saying what you think because, if you do, the chances are terrifically high of it backfiring badly and making everything worse. It can be hard to resist the temptation, but it's the wisest thing to do for everyone concerned – including your grandchildren. The way you handle it right from the start can have enormous, far-reaching implications.

It's easy to speak your mind in a way that precipitates a row, rather than preventing one. When Tiffany and Hamish split up, Hamish's widowed mother, Ada, dived right in with disastrous consequences. Ada recalls:

I've always been one to say what I think, and when Tiffany and Hamish told me they were divorcing, I'm afraid I let rip. I said they should try harder at their marriage. They had twin ten-year-old boys, for goodness sake, what about them? My grandsons deserved their parents to make every effort. I'm old-fashioned, I believe marriage should be for life – something you work at. It isn't all going to be a bed of roses, but you have to take the rough with the smooth. I said all this, and Hamish took it very well, really – he knows what I think. But Tiffany went crackers. She said I was accusing her of being selfish, that it was nothing to do with me and I should keep out of it.

When they divorced, she took the kids off to the other end of the country where her parents live, and I didn't see those boys for well over eighteen months. Hamish gets to visit them regularly, I will say that for her, but at first she stipulated that he didn't take them to visit *me*. It would have been hard for him to do that anyway, because he usually went down south to see them, and I was up here in Scotland. He did let them phone me, though, when they were with him. They used to tell me how much they missed me. After all, they weren't babies, they knew what they wanted – their gran. I missed *them* too. In the end Hamish persuaded Tiffany to let him bring them up for a week in the summer. I hardly ever talk to Tiffany, but I do see the boys two or three times a year now, and we phone each other quite a lot. We get by.

Ada's outburst was no doubt prompted by concern and disappointment, but it led to her losing her grandsons for almost two years. If she'd been able to control herself, who knows, maybe Tiffany wouldn't have rushed off to the South Coast. And even if she had decided to go back to her family, keeping everything on a friendly basis would have made her much more likely to allow the children to see their grandma – arrangements could have been put in place from the start.

This seems especially likely because Hamish and Tiffany managed to stay on friendly terms with each other.

Ada's outburst could also have spoiled things for Hamish. It would have been very easy for Tiffany to take his mother's attitude out on *him*. Ada's lucky, too, that her grandsons cared enough about her, and were old enough, to pressure their mother into letting them see her. Speaking your mind so aggressively can be risky. In this case it didn't just cost Ada tears, it also hurt her grandsons: they spent all that time without *her*, as well as without their father. They'd lost a parent and a loved grandparent as well.

In any case, you can't project your own beliefs onto your children. *You* might be a devotee of the 'till death us do part' philosophy, but if your children are having marital problems, then telling them they're 'failing' isn't going to help. You need to keep a sense of balance, and this can be very hard to do. Adrienne and Rory's son Jordan lived in Canada with his family. He divorced three years ago, but everyone has stayed on reasonable terms. Adrienne says:

> We realised there was some strain between our son and his wife, Debbie, but we were knocked sideways when he told us he was leaving her and their two boys, who were three and five at the time.
>
> We've always got on well with Debbie, and we went to Canada to see what we could do. We stayed with her because Jordan was living with friends, but we did spend time with both of them separately. They wanted to talk, and we just listened. We tried hard not to interfere – we were very conscious of the risks. They treated us as a sounding board because they both knew what they said to us wouldn't be repeated to the other one. Rory and I did suggest they try some counselling, but after eighteen months, they divorced.

They share custody of the children and we visit them all a couple of times a year. Luckily, Jordan and Debbie don't criticise each other to the boys – I can't imagine anything more cruel and wasteful. Our son is still very bitter, but we don't get into those conversations with him; we're not going to go down that road. He's married again, and Debbie has a new partner, too. We asked her where *we* stood, now there are step-grandparents, but she made it clear we're still their grandparents – that they all want us, which was a huge relief. But it's a fine line we walk.

Instead of forcing their views on Debbie and Jordan, Adrienne and Rory didn't judge and respected their privacy, so they both felt it was safe to confide their feelings – something that must have helped them cope in the thick of the divorce. If Adrienne and Rory had taken sides, or reported back between the two, they could have made an already bad situation intolerable, and racked up the tension and anger to boiling point. They earned the couple's trust and, as a result, they're all still on good terms.

Sometimes, being a long way apart can help you decide how to react to your children's divorce. Liam and Petra live in New Zealand with their three-year-old daughter. They're currently separated and in the process of getting a divorce. Liam's parents, Lavinia and Aidan, are in the UK, and trying to stay calm. Lavinia says:

Petra has a lot of family in New Zealand, but Liam's is over here. He phones us, saying he's desperate. He says, 'I've got nobody.' He wants us to go out there for a few weeks, but we feel we can't. We think they have to sort it out between them – it's a gut feeling. If we just arrived in the middle of everything, we might make it worse. We try to put it into perspective: maybe we're better out of it for the moment, while it's still so raw. Besides, Aidan's rather cross with Liam and, I think, if we were there, he might let this show.

Despite the distance, Petra's always been very good at keeping in touch, but she hasn't talked to us since they split up. That's a bit scary. She did text me once, right at the beginning, to say we'd always be part of our granddaughter's life, and that she'd talk to us soon, but she never has. It's been three months now and we've heard nothing. I've phoned her a few times, but she hasn't replied and I'm afraid of her thinking I'm a nuisance, so I daren't do it too often. I tell myself she's got a lot on her plate. I keep thinking about my granddaughter – she's only three – but I try not to let it take over my mind. If Petra can cope better without talking to us right now – if it helps her – then that's good. This separation is a fact, and we have to get used to it. It's out of our control.

I say this, but I'm trying to rationalise. I know that if they were in the UK, I'd have offered to take the baby while they sorted everything out. I'm just looking forward to a time when she's old enough to talk on the phone, and know who we are.

It's tough for Lavinia and Aidan. They're trying to keep things on an even keel by staying away, but they're feeling very isolated. It was thoughtful of Petra to contact them straight away to reassure them, but it's a pity she hasn't found time for just one follow-up call to put their minds at rest. She probably isn't worrying about what anyone else might be suffering; her own problems will occupy all her attention. Lavinia and Aidan are trying to think longer term, and they know that, because Liam and Petra plan to share custody, they won't lose touch permanently with their granddaughter.

At the same time, though, they should be aware that young children have very short memories, so it's important not to leave it *too* long.

How you react to the news of your child's divorce, will depend heavily on your relationship with them. Bruce and Suzanne were living in Italy when their daughter Elsa began to have problems with her marriage. She has three children. Suzanne says:

I started to think something was up between them, but nothing was said. Then Elsa had an operation, and when I came home to look after her and the children, she opened up about it. But she made me promise not to tell Bruce. I didn't, but eventually she told us both that she was thinking of leaving her husband.

We'd been in Italy for ten years but when we heard that, we decided to come back home for good. We wanted to be on the spot for Elsa and the children. I'm not absolutely sure she'd have made the break if we hadn't, although she didn't *ask* us to come home. Our granddaughter Matilda moved with her mother, and the two boys stayed with their father – that was how the children wanted it.

We haven't always found it easy to get on with our son-in-law and, to be frank, we're not really surprised all this happened, but everyone is still friendly. We make an effort – we manage. There's no question that Elsa is happier, and that's helpful for Matilda, who's told me she's glad about the divorce, because of the difference it's made to her mum. We see a lot of the boys, too. On the whole, it's worked out for the best.

Suzanne and Bruce didn't hesitate – they upped sticks and moved back to the UK to be with their daughter and grandchildren, but they didn't interfere. They made things better, not worse. They had a view, but didn't share it.

If your sympathies are *not* with your child, this can put you in a very delicate situation. When Kay left her husband, Jim, and took their baby son, her mother-in-law, Ethel, sympathised with her, but she kept quiet.

> I knew she was in the right. Jim hadn't been grown-up enough to be a husband and father. When they split, Kay pushed Jim away. She didn't allow him, or me, to bond with the baby. I could understand how she felt. She knew I agreed with her about Jim, but I was in the middle and trying to bridge the gap. I didn't see my grandson for a while, and I thought I'd lost him, but then Kay started visiting me. She would bring the baby every Sunday. She wanted Jim back. I could see it, and she told me so. She wanted me to help her, but I knew it wouldn't work out. I love my son, but I know his faults.

After the divorce, Kay took herself and her baby away, like a mother gathering her cubs round her in times of danger. That she re-established contact with her mother-in-law when she realised she wanted her husband back could be regarded cynically but, in fact, it's a sign that she liked and trusted Ethel. Kay knew it would be safe to approach her – that she would be welcomed. Ethel, in turn, was wise not to attempt to mend matters between her son and his wife. If she had and it had come to grief, she might have been blamed for it. She knew her own child, and could see it wasn't a realistic hope. By being honest, but refusing to take an active role between them, she's succeeded in maintaining contact with her daughter-in-law.

But what if the row has nothing to do with your child's

relationship with their partner? What if it's their partner's relationship with *you* that's the problem? This happened to Bettina and Ron, when their son married Allegra. Bettina explains:

> She always seemed to be on the defensive – we could never get past the post with her at all. At first, we thought it was because she was seven years older than our son. We thought she was worried we might disapprove, but we didn't. They were twenty-eight and thirty-five, and it seemed to us they ought to know their own minds at that age. In any case, it wasn't our business. They wanted kids, but Allegra had to go through IVF a couple of times and, when her triplets were born, she was very possessive – she hardly let us touch them. Everything had to be just so. I said a couple of things – nothing much, but she took them the wrong way, and before we knew it, things got very chilly – even with our son. Then we lent our daughter some cash to help her set up a little business, and Allegra didn't like *that* very much. We knew she was slighting us all the time, and we were very upset that she was influencing our son against us. Who did she think she was?
>
> By the time the kids were two, we were walking on eggshells. I didn't think things could get much worse. But then my husband lost his temper with Allegra when she snapped at me for the umpteenth time one afternoon, and there was an almighty row. We all said things, and then Ron and I left.
>
> That was three years ago, and we've only seen the children about four times since then. I blame Allegra, not my son. He phones us, but we never get invited to visit them, and the kids don't really know us now. We send birthday and Christmas cards and presents, but for the past couple of years we've spent Christmas in the Caribbean. It upsets me

too much to stay here, and think of what we're missing. We hardly feel like grandparents at all.

This kind of thing can happen all too easily. If someone is feeling a bit insecure and vulnerable, a comment they wouldn't normally worry about is seen as a criticism. Primeval defensive aggression cuts in, hackles rise, and suddenly everyone's in a circle, snarling. Allegra probably *was* worried that her new in-laws regarded her as too old for their son, but Bettina and Ron suspected that. If they'd allowed that possibility to dictate their behaviour, concentrated on being supportive and bolstering her confidence, she might have been more inclined to let them in. Possessiveness is very understandable in Allegra's circumstances after her struggles to get pregnant – what new mother wouldn't be? Again, Bettina and Ron could have made allowances for this, but their tacit criticism left their son in the horrible position of having to choose between his wife and his parents. As far as the loan went, it really wasn't Allegra's business, but by this time, everybody had taken a stand, and once lines are drawn it can be very hard to retreat from them because so much pride is involved.

The situation might look hopeless, but there's still a way for everyone to come back from this, if Ron and Bettina are prepared to swallow their pride and make the first move – perhaps by inviting the family to come to them. They don't need to mention the loan, but as far as the original dispute is concerned, they could say, 'Look, we never meant to upset you. We were a bit miffed we didn't seem to be getting much hands-on stuff with the children. It's hard for new grandparents to sit on the sidelines. But it was hard for you, too, and we understand, now, how you felt. We were wrong about it. Can't we move on from this? We'd love to be more involved with the children – we miss you all, and there are lots of ways we could help you . . .' Because it really doesn't matter now whose fault it was and by being big enough to take some of the blame, they could heal the breach between all of them. They could, of course, explain how they felt and why they acted the way they did, but they'd need to be careful it doesn't sound defensive, or worse, turn into a string of accusations, and start it all off again. If they handle it calmly, straightforwardly and honestly, their son and his wife might well jump at the chance to become a family again.

Helping Your Grandchildren Cope

Divorce or remarriage can have a devastating effect on children. It doesn't matter whether they're toddlers or teenagers, the breakdown of that entity they know as mum-and-dad, constitutes the end of the world as hey know it. However uncomfortable their life has been up to this point, however much their parents have shouted at each other, or at them, whoever was wrong or right, the dismantling of their home is like a death. They grieve for its loss.

Being children, they'll show that grief in all kinds of ways, depending on their age: tantrums, depression, defiance, rage . . . Their parents might be too self-involved to notice, or to act on it if they do — and that's where you can come in.

Being There for Them

Just the very fact of your presence will have a reassuring effect on your grandchildren, especially if you treat them the way you've always done. Familiar relationships will help them deal with what's happening. They're more likely to open up to you and share their worries.

Arthur and Claire's son divorced three years ago, and shares custody of their children with his ex-wife, Andrea. Claire says:

> When the divorce happened, the children were three and
> five and it was arranged they'd spend half the week with
> their mum and half with their dad. The 'exchange' used to
> happen in a car park, and we'd sometimes be there. To see
> them coming towards us with their little suitcases nearly
> broke our hearts.
>
> Shared custody has a lot going for it, of course, but there
> are bad points, too. Both their parents have remarried, and
> the children have to live by two different sets of rules. Their
> step-mother is very strict. Their mum, on the other hand,
> isn't very hot on discipline. She works full-time and her
> home is always chaotic. As a result, they treat their stays with
> her as a free-for-all. I asked the elder one, Rowan, why they
> behave like that for their mum, and he shrugged and said,
> 'Because we're allowed.'
>
> Our granddaughter Jade is six now, and she seems to be
> taking it all in her stride – she's full of beans, absorbed in the
> moment – after all, she was only three when it happened.
> But Rowan's insecure. I know he's never given up hoping,
> even now, that his mum and dad will get together again.
> Once, when the children and their mum were staying with
> us, his dad was supposed to join us but couldn't make it.
> Rowan said, 'If Daddy had come, we'd have been like a
> family again.' He's very bright, and ahead of the other kids
> at school, but always getting into trouble. He bottles things
> up and it comes out in bad behaviour. His parents keep
> getting sent for by his teachers, to discuss him. I talk to
> Rowan, although I don't want to make a big issue of it, and
> I listen when he wants to tell me things but, because we live
> a long way away, we can't see them as much as we'd like.
> They come to stay for a couple of weeks in the summer,

and we'll just be getting to the point where he'll start to talk to me, when it's time for them to leave.

I shouldn't be concerned, but I am. They love their parents, but they have two sets they can manipulate. So they're vulnerable – they could fall between two stools. As they get older, I hope they'll come and spend time with us on their own. Our role is clear – to be there for them, and to make sure they know that.

The fact that they're not close by hasn't prevented Claire and Arthur from doing everything they can to give their grandchildren the security they need, and just knowing they're in the background will be giving the children some peace of mind. It's clear that Rowan feels he *can* talk to his grandmother – she's being patient, and the time will come when he'll open up to her.

But while being apart can add difficulties, being nearby doesn't necessarily make everything easy. Meredith and Dermot live a couple of miles from their daughter Cordelia who split up with her husband, Alfie, a year ago. Dermot says:

Alfie left our daughter, but he only moved two hundred yards further down their road. Our two grandchildren stay alternate weekends with him. Although we're so near, we actually spend less time with them now than we used to. Before the split, we'd see them at some point every weekend but now, when they're with their dad, he won't let them see us at all. He reckons the fault was all Cordelia's, and he blames us, too, just for being her parents. He's very bad-tempered and glum, and he takes it out on the children and shouts at them, which we're not happy about, but we can't say anything. We try not to be judgemental.

He and Cordelia now have this semidetached relationship.

They occasionally spend the night at each other's houses, and even all go on holiday together. The children have keys to both houses, and seem to move fairly freely between the two. But there's a lot of tension. As a family, we've always spent Christmas Day together here, and this year they refused. Meredith was upset they wouldn't come, but I could understand it perfectly – a huge family 'do' would have been a nightmare for them, given what they were going through. Instead, they all went to Wales for a few days, and then Alfie left Cordelia there alone while he took the kids to stay at his parent's house in Lancashire. Cordelia had been warned off, so she couldn't go with them.

The grandchildren are just about coping, but we'd love to do more to help them. Our elder granddaughter is fourteen, and getting very grown-up. She's more interested in her friends than her grandparents, but she does open up to my wife. She can't talk to her dad, because they argue. She hated all the rows and shouting before the split, but I don't think she's much happier now, and, on top of that, she's confused and self-conscious, experiencing all the things every adolescent goes through. It doesn't help that she's getting a bit overweight – hardly surprising, given what they've been eating over the last year. The younger girl is only twelve, but in many ways she's had to grow up in a very short time, and fend for herself. We're a little bit worried. The other day, I found her at home on her own in the middle of the morning – just sitting there. I wonder, is she missing school? Cordelia goes to work early so it would be easy to kid her. I didn't question her at the time, and her mum believes she stayed at home because she was a bit off-colour. Apparently, she's doing well at school, but her sister thinks she's bunking off.

Life is chaotic for our grandchildren. We're here – steady, unchanging – they can come round and see us at any time, but we've never articulated that in so many words. Perhaps we should.

There's a lot to think about here. Dermot's instinct is right – it would be a good idea to talk to their granddaughters. They don't need to make a big solemn performance of it – just a rather casual chat when they're together one day, and safe from parental interruption, to reassure them that whatever happens, they'll always love them; that if they're ever worried, or upset, or just need to let off steam, they can come and talk; that no time is the wrong time; that it's *safe*; that they'll listen, not lecture. Something like, 'You know we're always here. Don't worry, you can tell us *anything*.' The children might already know this deep down, but sometimes things need saying out loud.

Their elder granddaughter might be becoming more sophisticated but at fourteen she's still half a child, and there will be feelings she's not showing. And if their younger granddaughter *is* truanting, or on the brink, then it needs to be nipped in the bud quickly. It would help her to talk about what she's feeling, without accusations or blame. Understanding is what's called for, and her grandparents are the perfect people to provide it because they're not part of the cause of her unhappiness.

Dermot and Meredith are tending to let things drift, because they're afraid of interfering, but diffidence isn't always the best approach. There's more at stake here than their daughter's feelings. In any case, they could talk to her, too, about what's worrying them; ask her what *she's* thinking and feeling; show her that she has their love and support – that she doesn't have to handle all this alone. And they could try to spend more time with their grandchildren, to foster trust – maybe find things they could do together – new interests, trips out to places or events they'd enjoy. In the aftermath of a split, children can be in a bit of a vacuum, and they might welcome any line that's thrown them.

Sometimes, the best help you can give as grandparents is simply to set a good example. Silas and Myrtle's son Errol divorced Carina, and remarried less than a year afterwards. His two sons were having trouble getting on with their new step-mother. Myrtle says:

> Carina went back to her family in Jamaica, and Errol got custody of the children, so when he married Dana so quickly, our grandsons, who were five and six, found it very hard to cope. Dana's one of those women who doesn't give a lot – she's very buttoned up, and I think the kids were put off by that. I have to say we were, too. We'd loved Carina, who was a sweetie, and we found it hard to get to know Dana.
>
> The boys would play her up and then come round to our house and moan about her. We used to say, she's your mum now, you have to get used to her, and give them a cuddle. They weren't getting many of those from her. We don't think she meant to be unkind, but her style was just so different from Carina's. One day the youngest boy came running in with a bad cut on his leg, but instead of kissing him better, Dana gave him a lecture about not jumping off the wall. I wanted to shout at her, 'He's a little kid – love him!' Silas and I do criticise her to each other, and though we've been careful not to say anything in front of the kids, I guess they know how we feel.
>
> It's been two years, now, and Dana's softened a bit, but the fact is she'll never be like Carina. The kids get on with her better, but you can tell they don't *really* love her. Errol sees it, of course.

What's happened here is a great pity. The children were missing their mother. Dana was the interloper who'd taken their mother's place, and however she behaved, they'd have resented her for it. This is a hard situation to be in. It's possible that Dana was simply trying not to muscle in on them. Maybe she felt that if she swept in and 'mothered' them, they'd resent her even more, and she knew how much everyone had loved her predecessor. It was a case of 'follow that'.

Myrtle and Silas could have done a lot to smooth the transition, both for their grandsons and for Dana herself. Of course she isn't the same as Carina – they're different people with different personalities, and nothing can change that.

But by understanding the position she was in, and supporting both her and Errol, they'd have shown her that, as far as they were concerned, she was part of the family. A little bit of warm family feeling would have gone a long way towards making everyone relax, and that would have rubbed off on the boys. Children of their age *do* pick up on bad vibes – but they'll follow a lead, and they're young enough to live for the moment. They probably do love Dana by now, even though the relationship may never be quite the same as with their mother.

There are other practical ways you can help your children and grandchildren. Davina and Conan's daughter separated from her husband two years ago. Conan recalled: 'Half term was coming up, so we offered to take our two grandchildren, who were thirteen and eight, to the coast for a few days. We always have them for a while in the school holidays, and it seemed like a good plan to carry on as usual. While we were there we didn't discuss their situation at all – we behaved as if everything was normal, to take their minds off it. They didn't bring it up, either, though they were both a bit subdued. The eight-year-old seemed more able to switch to enjoyment; he was happy playing in the sea and sand. Our granddaughter spent all her time on the phone, texting her friends.'

As a teenager, their granddaughter was probably finding consolation and support in this contact with her peers. She wasn't necessarily talking about what was happening in her family, just the usual chatter would be comforting – something about her life that was familiar. They'd both have benefited from being away from the centre of things, even though it was only for a few days. Davina and Conan weren't trying to pretend that nothing untoward was happening, simply giving them the opportunity to think about something else for a while – taking the heat off them.

For children, whatever their age, watching the two most important people in their lives falling out of love and into enmity, is a frightening experience on many levels, facing them with a lot of questions about their own role in this disintegration. For one thing, there's the problem of divided loyalty. Should they take sides? Do they *want* to take sides? If the answer to the latter is yes, then they'll worry about that, too. They love both their parents, and will beat themselves up about favouring one over the other. On the other hand, if the answer is no, then does that mean they're a bad person? And they might feel guilty, wondering, 'Is it me? Is it *my* fault they're not getting on?' This may not be very logical, but it is natural, especially if there are a lot of rows to listen to.

Youngsters aren't necessarily going to come out with any of this – they're much more likely to keep it hidden, because they're worried about what the answers might say about them. By taking them away from the red-hot core of the problem, even for a short time, grandparents can give them some space to be themselves. It doesn't have to be a full-on holiday. Just the occasional break – a casual lunch, a couple of hours at a football match, or the cinema, will provide some relief.

Keeping Them in Your Life

If you're prevented from seeing your grandchildren after their parents divorce, everyone suffers – them, you, even your child's ex who loses your support and help. But the situation can be complex. Sometimes, the existence of 'new' grand-parents – that is, step-grandparents, can mean you're seen as surplus to requirements.

This happened to Neville and Olwen when their son divorced and his ex-wife remarried. Olwen says: 'We'd managed to stay on reasonable terms with our daughter-in-law, but when she remar-ried, everything changed. His parents were around all the time, and no one seemed to want us. We live quite a way from them, so we couldn't just pop in – we had to invite ourselves, or wait to be invited. They didn't need us, and gradually we just got squeezed out of their lives.' It's easy to see why a new family unit might not want, or need, outsiders, whose presence in their lives might make it more difficult for the step-grandparents to form a bond with the children. But it's a pity that how the children feel hasn't been taken into consideration. They're missing 'their' grandparents, and that could make their own adjustment to the new circumstances all the harder.

Access – What the Law Says

Unfortunately, under the law, you have no *right* of access. This default position is there to cover the situations where isola-tion from family is the right thing. No one can argue that those situations don't exist, but the law needs to be applied with intelligence. In theory, the idea is to protect children by preventing unnecessary disruption in their lives, but in practice, it can be administered without regard to how close a bond you have with your grandchildren, or how important a part of their lives you are or have been.

Under the Children Act 1989, the parent(s) with responsibility for your grandchild has the right to deny you access. They may truly believe it's best for the child. But equally, if you've fallen out for some reason, or your child's ex-spouse has custody after a messy divorce and wants to take it out on you, the law makes it easy. If you feel access is being wrongly denied you, you should start by talking to the parent(s) and trying to resolve it that way. If this doesn't work, a second route is mediation through social services. Under the Children Act, they must 'promote contact' with a child's family, which includes grandparents, unless it's deemed to be actively harmful or otherwise inconsistent with the child's welfare (in which case, they can turn you down out of hand). They must take the child's wishes into account, too. Should all this fail, you can go to court to attempt to obtain a contact order, which would require the responsible parent(s) to allow you contact with your grandchild.

It's not straightforward. For a start, you can't simply apply for contact. With a few exceptions, you have to apply for *permission* to apply. This sounds mad, but it's there to prevent gratuitous applications by people who might not be good for the child. Whether that precaution should be standard in the case of grandparents is a somewhat debatable point. You'll need to fill in forms and show you won't be disrupting your grandchild's life. If they grant you permission to apply for contact, then you'll have to present all kinds of evidence to back up your claim that contact with you will be good for your grandchild. The process then includes at least one hearing (see pages 271–2). You'll need a solicitor who's an expert in this field. There are cases where grandparents have lost everything – including their home – to finance their attempt to gain access to their grandchildren. Applying to the court should be a last resort – it's expensive (solicitors' fees, court fees, etc.).

If contact is awarded, it will be either direct or indirect. The former is face-to-face, the latter might be the right to send letters and parcels, make phone calls or send emails. In some cases, the court will leave it to the people involved and/or the local authority to determine the frequency, etc., but in others, the court makes the decision. As with all these issues, decisions are made subjectively, which is as it should be, but with greater or lesser sensitivity, depending on the quality and priorities of local social services. The law could vary regionally and procedures will certainly vary locally, so it's best to do some homework before you start. If you're not happy with the way things are handled, or the results, you can complain (see pages 271–2).

If you do succeed in getting a contact order, the parents might still not allow you to see your grandchild. In these circumstances, the court can fine them, and the last resort is a prison sentence – but that would very rarely happen.

Getting It Right

There's significant research to show that children cope better during the trauma of divorce, or family break-up, when they've had the benefit of constant contact with loving grandparents. They deal with the stress, disruption, unhappiness and insecurity more effectively. It sounds self-evident, doesn't it? But it can be a difficult call. There's more than one side to most stories and the law has to cover a huge variety of situations.

Sadie has two girls, now aged ten and seven. Her mother, Joan, interfered heavily in her marriage, and again after Sadie was divorced, three years ago.

My mum was the cause of a lot of our problems — she meddled all the time, and when we broke up she backed my husband to the hilt, not me. She always thought I should get back together with him and told me so — often.

Then I got married again, and Mum didn't get on with Bradley, my new husband. She preferred my ex, and was always making trouble. We kept having rows, and they got so bad I finally told her she couldn't see the children so often and that when she did, it would have to be without me — I couldn't bear to talk to her. The kids did keep on seeing her, but she said dreadful things about me, and told the children I'd said she might not be able to see them again. They used to come home in tears. My eldest daughter said, 'Nanny says if we lived with her, everything would be all right. We want to live with Nanny.' She was only seven. We had to warn their school not to let my mum pick them up, because we were worried she'd take them home with her. And the girls would play us off against each other. Mum used them to make me doubt myself — there were times when I wondered if I *was* a bad mother, for leaving their dad.

Then she told us she was taking us to court for more access. It came right out of the blue. We couldn't afford a solicitor. The whole thing was appalling. We were interviewed — they even wanted to interview the girls. Eventually, she was granted access for one day and one overnight a month. Since then, it's settled down, and things have improved now the girls are older. But they're still a bit anxious around their grandma. It's bound to have affected them.

Still, she's my mum, and I've never imagined life without her, even when things were at their worst. We've forgiven her and, in spite of everything, we do still want her involved. I didn't have any grandparents, and it's going to be different for my kids.

In this case, the court felt it needed to make sure Joan maintained contact with her granddaughters, and Sadie, although she was justifiably angry with her mother, has accepted this, so things have got better for all of them.

As a grandparent, you might believe that you should have an automatic right to see your grandchildren: you're their flesh and blood, they're part of you, and nothing can change that. You might well feel that the default position should be right of access, only to be withheld in special circumstances. But your children might not see it that way. Leanne has three boys under ten. Her husband's parents are both divorced and remarried. She says: 'If I split up with my husband there's no way I'd let my father-in-law see the kids. I'd be worried he'd influence them, set them against me, undermine me. I don't like the way he undermines me *now*, giving them big bags of sweets and whispering, "Don't tell your mum." He once smacked my eldest – I was livid – absolutely furious. He had no right to touch my child. And these days, with all these remarriages where one grandparent isn't even related to the grandchildren, I'm sure they don't care so much about them – they genuinely don't want to be bothered. I don't think grandparents should have any rights of access. They're *my* children, and I should decide who they see.'

What Leanne says is harsh, but try to imagine the situation she describes. Cast your mind back to the time when *your* children were small. Imagine you had a vitriolic split with your partner – that you really hated each other. Be honest with yourself – would parental possessiveness kick in, and might you worry that his/her parents would try to influence your children, or even go so far as to blacken you to them? Leanne's view is uncompromising, but she isn't alone in feeling like this.

Fair enough, but it does leave the way wide open for

revenge, as Bethany and Donald found, when their son Kent and his wife, Isla, divorced. Donald says:

When Kent and Isla broke up it was like World War Two. We've never seen so much anger. She had a filthy temper, and they fought like cat and dog. Their two kids were caught in the middle, watching their mum and dad shrieking at each other. We used to try to talk the pair of them down, and it sometimes worked with our son, but Isla would turn on us and shout her head off. Then Kent found a girlfriend and ran off with her. It didn't surprise us at all. We wondered how he'd stuck it so long. Isla came round and yelled at us from the front garden. She called Kent all the names under the sun and said we'd never see the kids again. We hoped it was just anger talking, because when all the fighting had been going on, we'd had the kids a lot to get them out from under it. They'd got used to coming round after school for their tea, and staying as long as we thought they could get away with. We never said anything critical about Isla to the boys – although we were pretty fed up with her carryings on.

When the divorce came through she sent us a really nasty email, saying she and the boys never wanted to see us again; we were just like Kent, and we'd be a bad influence on them. That was rich, considering how she'd behaved. But we tried to talk her out of it. We emailed and phoned her – we even begged. We hated to think the children would believe we didn't care about them. None of it worked, though. She was taking out her spite on us – she enjoyed it, we think. Kent had to go to court to get access to his own children. Social services didn't want him to have it, because they were afraid that if he and Isla were together in the same room, the rows would upset the children. It was stupid, because they were much more upset at never seeing their father or us. I think Bethany and I were the only stable people in their lives.

Luckily, the court agreed with Kent, although Isla makes it as difficult as possible for him. But his access order didn't help *us*, because she won't let us see the kids at all. We can't go to court: it cost Kent £7,000, and we don't have that kind of money. Kent would like to bring them round to us when they're with him, but he doesn't want to jeopardise his own position and, anyway, we don't think it would be good for the children to have to pretend, or lie, or face their mum's anger if she found out. It's all hopeless, really.

This is a truly horrible situation for Bethany and Donald and their grandchildren. Isla was hurt, so she wanted to hit out at her husband in any way she could. His parents, who, she was sure, were on his side, were the perfect target. The maelstrom of feelings unleashed when a marriage breaks up can mean that people who might in normal circumstances be generous, unselfish, considerate, become the opposite: self-obsessed, even paranoid, resentful, completely selfish. If everything you value is falling round your ears, you're likely to put yourself first in the belief that no one else is going to. It's self-preservation, and it's one way of getting you through the worst patches. But it's very destructive for everyone. Bethany and Donald are helpless to act until Isla's anger cools down and she feels less vengeful, less inclined to lash out. This might happen, and if they're patient they might find things improve. At least, in their case, their son will keep their image fresh in the children's minds.

If you find yourself faced with the break-up of your child's marriage, try very hard to remain on reasonable terms with their spouse, and establish a relationship that stands alone.

You're separate people, not an extension of your children. This doesn't mean you need to 'betray' your own child, or be disloyal. What it does mean is talking to both of them separately, and explaining what you're trying to do. To your child, you can say, 'Look, we know how you both feel about each other, but we'd like to keep on seeing our grandchildren, so we want you to know, that although we'll try to be on good terms with him/her, we'll never take sides against you, or criticise you.' To your child's ex, you could say, 'We really love our grandchildren – and you know they love us. It would be such a pity if the fact that you and their mum/dad don't love each other any more, prevents them from having *us*, as well. We promise never to say anything about our son/daughter to them if you don't want us to, and we'll never, never, criticise you to the children. Trust us, and we won't let you down.' Having said this, you'll need to stick to it, of course. It's worth a shot – think of what you've got to lose.

But the desire to punish can extend to other kinds of family rift, too. When Adelaide married Wesley, his son Rupert couldn't forgive him – with disastrous consequences. Adelaide explains: 'Rupert didn't want his dad to marry me. He and his girlfriend, Juliet, had a baby daughter. Rupert wasn't working, and Wesley gave him money. He took the money, but we didn't see the baby. After a year, I went round and knocked on the door. Juliet answered it, and she let me in. I said, "You've never given me the chance to be a grandma." She cried, and told me she was pregnant again. I occasionally saw her and the two girls after that, but Wesley wouldn't forgive Rupert. He said he didn't want to know anything about his son.' This is so sad for everyone. Rupert was jealous of his father's new wife, and Wesley, quite naturally, resented that. Maybe if they'd been able to talk about it, instead of letting it go on, the four of them could have established some kind of relationship. The fact that Juliet allowed her step-mother-in-law back into her life shows that this might have been possible.

It's frighteningly easy to get into habits that can seem impossible to break. If you get used to having certain feelings about a member of your family, you can go for years without questioning these feelings. But what happens if the person dies? You're left with unfinished business – an unhappy ending you can never change. The time might come when you'd give anything to alter it. It's been said that 'if only' are the saddest words in the English language and, in this context at least, it's true.

The Adoption Complication

Adoption is another bogeyman that can raise its head to plague the parents of divorced children. If your child gets divorced, doesn't have custody of your grandchildren, and the parent who does remarries, the new step-parent might well want to adopt them as his/her own. It's easy to understand why: it makes them a 'proper' family, because it transfers to the step-parent all the legal rights that their other birth parent had – in other words, parental responsibility. So *your* child will no longer have any legal rights over his/her children.

This affects you directly, because if your child can't see the children, then you probably won't be able to, either. In fact, you may lose all contact, even if your child doesn't. You can be out on a limb. You're left with no rights at all, just as if your grandchildren had been adopted by two 'strangers' (see Chapter 5 and pages 264–5, plus pages 271–2). This happened to Glenys and Percy, when their son Sam divorced. Percy says:

Our daughter-in-law Bridget was pretty awful during the

divorce. Not that you can blame her, really – Sam had been having an affair. But she wouldn't let him, or us, near the children at all. The boys were two and four when it all happened. We had hoped that she'd at least let *us* see them. After all, we hadn't done anything to her, and the boys were used to spending quite a lot of time with us, but no, she wasn't having it.

Then, eighteen months later, she married this chap, and they decided they wanted him to adopt the boys. Bridget told Sam it was because they wanted everyone to have the same surname, but there are other ways to do that. We think she did it out of spite, to cut Sam out completely.

During that time we made a lot of attempts to stay friends with her, and she always refused to have anything to do with us, but anyway, we thought we'd better make one last try. It was no-go. She said we were part of the past – a past she wanted to forget, and that they were better off without us. It just about broke Glenys's heart. We tried sending parcels at Christmas, but they all got sent back – they'd never even been opened. The boys are seven and five now – they wouldn't know us if they saw us.

Percy and Glenys could apply to the court for access to their grandsons, but it's unlikely, at this late date, that they'd be given it (see pages 271–2). The children might not now remember their grandparents at all. What's more, the court, rightly or wrongly, must have felt that adoption was the best thing in this case, and that might well work against Percy and Glenys, too. They still have the option of applying to be put on their grandsons' contact register, for when they're older. There's a good chance the children will want to pursue their roots and background by then.

Not all divorced couples are so antagonistic towards each

other (or the respective families), but the lesson to be learned from this terrible experience is not to let too much time pass. In general, the best way to keep contact is to keep talking.

KEEPING THE PEACE

Don't

Interfere by telling your children what to do.

Give advice unless you're asked for it.

Lecture them on their responsibilities.

Take sides or criticise one to the other.

Tell one spouse what the other has said to you.

Lose your temper.

Do

Listen to them.

Treat what they tell you in confidence.

Tell them they can trust you – and mean it.

Be understanding – make allowances.

Be supportive of both sides in their stress, regardless of your
own views.

HELPING YOUR GRANDCHILDREN

Don't

Report their conversations with you to their parents.

Criticise either of their parents to them.

Take sides.

Show any anger you feel.

Do

Be there for them.

Show them they can trust you.

Make allowances for bad behaviour.

Be loving and calm.

Listen to them.

Do things with them to distract them from the tension.

Be above the fight.

Keep a careful eye on their emotional state.

What to Say to Them

You can tell me *anything* – always.

I'll always be here for you.

I'll always love you.

Your mum and dad still love *you*, even though they don't love each other.

It's not your fault.

8

As They Grow Older

The classic image of grandparents and grandchildren is of a couple of nice old dears in cardigans, cuddling or smiling fondly at nice little children – cute babies, lively toddlers, charming five-year-olds. These days, of course, those old people are more likely to be fairly with-it middle-aged people in jeans and in fashionable haircuts, but the children are still small and sweet. It seems to be taken for granted that adolescents and grandparents are an unlikely combo; that by the time they've reached their teens, youngsters have lost interest in the older members of their family.

When our grandchildren are small, we're (comparatively)

young, so it's relatively easy to be the brightest star in their firmament. We can dazzle them, sweep them off their Start-rites with our dedication to their pleasure. It's a doddle. We're up for it, and they're panting for it – a match made in heaven.

But as they get older, things begin to change; *they* begin to change. Trips that used to wow them, to the swings or the petting zoo, lose their appeal. The puzzles, toys and other treats that delighted them don't cut the mustard any longer. The bedtime stories they loved you to read to them, even after they began to read for themselves, become surplus to requirements. They're devouring Harry Potter and Philip Pullman without any help from you. They've moved on. Instead of a jigsaw, they pore over their PlayStation; they wield a mobile phone rather than a paintbrush; their musical tastes have gone from nursery rhymes and silly songs to Indie, rap and other, more obscure (at least, to you), genres. It happens gradually, but suddenly you look round and realise they're growing up, have sophisticated tastes, and a whole raft of new friends to hang out with; friends who don't know *you* at all, and don't especially want to. From being at the core of their clique, you're not even in it any more.

You look at them with awe, and not a little trepidation, remembering your tussles with their parents when *they* were teenagers: the angst, the raging hormones that turned your own little angels into the unknown and unknowable. It was a rocky road then, so now, thirty years later, what chance do you stand?

Your energy levels might still be amazing; you might be capable of all kinds of exciting physical activities your grand-children would love – but would they love to do them with *you*? You might be a technological wizard/computer buff, with a PC set-up that would be the envy of Bill Gates; you might own a Blackberry; download ring tones; be totally au fait with iPhones and iPods, mini-disc burners and Skype. But will they want to talk technology with *you*?

And if you're a great-grandparent, then you're probably even more convinced that your cool-factor has bottomed out. You're a dinosaur, for goodness sake. What could you possibly have to offer these shiny new almost-adults?

The answer is, a great deal. You don't stop loving people just because you get older, and neither will your grandchildren. You're key figures in their lives, and you don't cease to matter to them just because they no longer need your help to fasten buttons. Their dependency on your love and support, their trust that you're always on their team and the security this provides is fundamental to their development not just as children, but as adults, too.

Of course it's true that as they grow, you probably won't spend as much time with them as you used to. They're less likely to come for the weekend at the drop of a hat. They'll have other interesting things to do. That's natural. And life sticks its oar in, too. College, gap years, jobs, will take them away – but physically, not necessarily emotionally, unless you allow it to happen. It's in your power to keep the closeness. The relationship you've established with your grandchildren is a unique one. Throughout their lives, no one else will ever occupy the place you hold in their hearts.

Changing Roles

Time goes by, and the little faces that looked up so trustingly into yours, the little voices that called out 'Grandma!' from the garden or the loo, demanding – and indeed, expecting – your immediate attention, gradually change.

As your grandchildren gain independence and confidence, as they learn the skills of living, they seem to need you less and less. They can tie their own shoelaces – maybe you taught them how; they can shower alone; they can clean their own teeth. Time passes and you don't need to meet them from school; fast-forward again and they're discussing college places with their parents, or leaving school to start a job.

Where do you fit in to all this? *Don't* they need you any more? Of course they do. Pre-teens and teens might look and act like aliens (haven't they always?), but inside, they're the same people you've loved, and who've loved you from birth. They still need that love as they mature, because it's not just you who's finding it weird they're growing up – it's weird for *them*, too. If you're flexible about how you handle them, and adjust and adapt to their new circumstances, you can take your relationship to a new level. They'll learn to trust you in a deeper way because they'll be backing up their childhood habit with an adult reliance on you.

Being a Friend

Most adolescent and teenage tensions manifest themselves in some sort of clash with parental authority. Rows happen largely because, just like the 'terrible twos', they're pushing the boundaries, flexing their muscles, honing their personality to cope with the rigours of adult life. Their parents accuse them of being moody, or thoughtless, untidy, disrespectful . . . They accuse their parents of 'not understanding', of being too restrictive, demanding . . . These clashes, whatever their ostensible cause, are about power and control. The established generation wants to keep it; the upcoming generation needs to take it. It's a battle that's as old as time. Which means that, as when they were very small, you have an advantage over their parents, simply because you *aren't* their parents. This puts you in a crucial position – you can be the equivalent of 'time out' for both.

If your grandchildren want to talk, and know you'll listen without lecturing, without the ghost of the wagging finger that's an inevitable part of most discussions with their parents, then they'll talk to *you*. You can stand back and look at things in cold blood – after all, it's not your row. Jacob and Honour found this with their fourteen-year-old grandson, Gwyn. Honour says:

Gwyn's always been a little firebrand and, from being quite small, he's come running to us when he's had a falling-out with his mum or dad. We've usually been able to calm him down. Since he turned thirteen, he's had teen attitude with a vengeance. He'll flounce in, grunt something, and sit down in front of our TV. We tend to downplay it, not rush up and make a fuss. We just ignore his behaviour, and wait until he starts to talk. He always does! It's usually something tiny, like his mum getting at him for kicking his dirty clothes under the bed but, to hear him, you'd think he had two-headed monsters for parents! We're sometimes tempted to laugh, but we never do, although it can be hard to keep a straight face. Jacob or I might dredge up a similar story from our own teen days, and make us all smile. Or I might grin and say, 'Well, *I* wouldn't want to go hunting under your bed for stinky socks, either – yuk!' But we don't criticise him, and we never take sides. We see our job as being there to defuse the situation, so he goes home in a calmer frame of mind. We're his safety valve, I think, and glad to be.

Honour and Jacob are right not to laugh at Gwyn, or belittle his worries. It's important to take your grandchildren seriously as people – they may not yet be fully fledged grown-ups, but their problems are real – and enormous – to them. Remember how you felt at that age: the world is against you; no one understands. They're his refuge – he knows it's safe. He can let off steam and they still love him. Sometimes, in the heat of hormones, it can be hard to remember that about your parents. Gwyn's aware his grandparents won't side with him, he's had years of experience as to how they behave, but he also knows they won't tell him off.

It's vital to stay one step removed. Your grandchildren need to know they can talk to you without it all going back to their parents. And, in turn, their parents need to feel they can trust you not to undermine them. They're having a hard enough job teen-grappling as it is, without you doing a 'good cop, bad cop' number on them.

Gideon discovered this to his cost, when his grandson Jonas was thirteen.

Jonas came to me in a terrible temper one day, saying his mum and dad were being unfair – they wouldn't let him go on a school skiing trip. He raged around a bit and said his sister had gone on holiday with her class – why couldn't he? I said he'd need to talk to them about it – maybe they couldn't afford to pay for it. Then I made my big mistake, I told him if they hadn't the money, I'd pay for him to go. He brightened up and went straight home to tell his parents that 'Granddad said he could go skiing'. Within seconds they were on the phone to me, furious. What did I think I was doing? Did I think they'd be so unfair as to not treat the two of them the same? There hadn't been a school trip planned for his class, so they'd bought Jonas a new sound system he'd been wanting. It was only now, when the skiing season was coming up, he realised he was missing something. He'd thrown a huge strop when they'd said he couldn't go. My son and his wife said I couldn't pay for the holiday – that Jonas needed to be taught money doesn't grow on trees, and that banging about in a temper like a petulant child, wasn't going to get him anywhere. They told me I'd let them down and gone behind their backs – and they were hurt I could believe they were being mean. I felt a complete fool, falling for the ravings of a thirteen-year-old.

Of course, I hadn't thought they were mean, just perhaps a bit hard-up and too embarrassed to tell me. I said I was sorry, and I had a word with Jonas, too. He looked a bit shamefaced but, you know, I think he thought less of me – not for backing out of paying for the trip, but for falling for it in the first place. I'm a bit wiser now.

Gideon has learned the hard way that teenagers can be just as selfish as two-year-olds – it's that survival instinct at work again, rolling over everything in its path. He's realised too, that it's best to check up before you make that sort of promise. There might be another side to the story.

But if you play it sensitively, you can be a big help to both sides, especially if you're able to open your grandchildren's minds to the bigger picture. Again, you're not part of the problem, so you're well-placed to do this. Where their parents, anxious, or upset, might have a rant, *you* can point out gently, without accusations, what it might feel like to be the other person. For example, you could ask them to imagine how worried their Mum and Dad must have been, sitting up late, not knowing where they were, when a quick phone call would have sorted it. Give them something to think about, encourage them to question their motives.

You can open their parents' minds too; arguments can easily flare up because, upset at what they see as defiance, parents have forgotten what it feels like to be a teenager and how things might seem from their children's point of view. That's not to say they're in the wrong, or that they have no reason to get angry, it's just the old communication problem once again. Take the classic teen–parent rows about doing their share, tidying their rooms, etc. Parents tell their children to do it – they either don't do it or put it off, perhaps intending to do it, so parents ask again, and maybe again, become increasingly irritated and start shouting. Then their children shout back, accuse them of nagging: 'You're always on at me, leave me alone.' Parents come back with, 'You never do anything I tell you – you're a slob, you're selfish. It's not our job to pick up after you . . .' Sounds familiar, doesn't it?

And then there's the moodiness. Teenagers veer between incredible highs, when they're full of energy (and correspondingly loud), and terrible lows, when it's as much as they can do to grunt, when everything and everybody makes them want to lash out, whether it's deserved or not. They can't help these moods – it's a direct result of hormonal imbalance, and they're as much victims as you are.

Parents are too close to all these issues – they have to live with them every day, and they let it get to them. You, on the other hand, are out of the loop. You can keep your calm, remind your children what *they* used to be like, and ask them what would have worked for them at the time. You can suggest that, instead of just getting mad, there might be other ways to tackle things. It might not effect a revolution, but it will make them more aware of the gruesome realities of being a teenager.

There's no need to get into the middle of a specific individual row. You can say, in general terms, without breaking a confidence, 'I don't know what you think, but it seems to me that . . .' or 'Have you thought of . . . ?' 'What do you think of . . . ?' or 'Do you remember when *you* did that?' As ever, you can't tell your children how to be parents, but you might be able to insert a thought or two for them to ponder on. But you're walking on razor blades here. Daphne's granddaughter Aisling visits her when she comes home from university. Daphne says:

My daughter's a single mum, so I had Aisling a lot when she was little, and we've always got on well. She did get a bit big for her boots as she got older, and rather bossy, but she was always fine with me as long as I didn't try to give her advice! Now she's at university, she's very good at popping in for a chat in the holidays.

In the Easter of her first year, she came round, and I thought she looked pale. She was definitely off-colour, and I asked her if she felt all right. I put my arm round her shoulders, and it seemed to be the signal she was waiting for – she broke down and started sobbing. Her boyfriend had split up with her; she'd got herself into a right state, and now she was behind with her work. She hadn't told her mum because although she knew she'd be sympathetic about the boyfriend, she thought she'd get bawled out about the work. And she didn't want to worry her. Her mother has always pushed Aisling to do well at college, because she had such a hard start herself.

I gave her some big hugs and asked how far behind she was. When she told me, I thought it didn't sound too bad. I asked her if she liked her tutor and she said he was OK, so I suggested she have a word with him – tell him she'd been a bit upset about something personal, and ask for some time to catch up. I said that colleges can be reasonable about that kind of thing, especially if she'd been doing all right before. As for the boyfriend – I told her she was bound to feel it, but if she let it interfere with her degree, then he'd won every way. Was he worth that? I didn't say he *wasn't*, she wouldn't have wanted to hear that — if she hadn't cared about him she'd never have got upset in the first place, would she? When you're nineteen, love can be painful. I did suggest she told her mum, though. I said that by telling her she planned to talk to the tutor, Aisling could put her mind at rest, so she wouldn't panic she was letting everything slide. But no, she wouldn't do it.

Anyway, she went back after Easter, sorted it out, and phoned me, sounding much happier. She's doing fine now, but her mum never did find out, and I still feel guilty about that. She'd be so hurt.

Daphne was in a tricky spot here. She did the right thing by suggesting Aisling talk to her mother, but she couldn't force her to do it, or break a confidence herself. You can only do your best. When it comes to the crunch, your grandchildren are individuals.

It's different if you have reason to believe that something is seriously wrong. If it's abuse that worries you, then you'll need to listen very carefully to what they're saying — or not saying (see Chapter 3). If it's alcohol, or drugs, or bullying, then again, listen, and invite confidence, but by your behaviour, not by pushing. Depending on what you suspect, or guess, you can say to them 'Look, if anything's bothering you, you know you can tell me. I'll love you no matter what it is.' This is a very delicate area, because you might not want to promise them that what they say won't go any further. And in any case, what you do about telling their parents will depend on your relationship, and your grandchildren's, with the latter. There are organisations to help you, and youngsters themselves, in these situations (see pages 257–8). The most important thing is to ensure your grandchildren know you'll be there for them, *whatever happens.*

Alban was faced with a difficult situation when he discovered that his fifteen-year-old granddaughter, Bryony, was taking drugs.

I knew my daughter had suspected for some time that Bryony was doing drugs. We were both worried to death. Then one day when she was with me, I smelled dope on her jacket. I said, 'That smells familiar. I remember it from college parties.' She tried to pass it off, but I said there was no point, I knew what it was. Her curiosity got the better of her and of course she wanted to know how I knew. Had *I* smoked dope? As it happened I had, but only once. I told her why it hadn't appealed, and asked her why she liked it. We had this strange, almost academic, conversation about cannabis, and all the time I was dying to grab her by her silly shoulders and shake some sense into her. I didn't tell Bryony she was on the slippery slope to perdition, or get mad and start to shriek – all of which I'm sure her mum wouldn't have been able to stop herself from doing. At the finish, though, I told her I loved her, but I couldn't condone it. I said she was breaking the law, and it worried me just as much as if she'd been ram-raiding, or shoplifting, or some other crime. If she carried on, I said, I'd be forced to tell her mum – maybe even the police – because I felt very strongly about it.

Bryony got on her high horse a bit and huffed on about it being no big deal, because her friends do it, but I hope what I said had weight because I'd been around in the drug-taking 1970s, and *I* hadn't followed my friends. That made me 'cooler', somehow. I'm keeping a close eye on her, and I hope she's going to stop. But I feel terrible not having told her mum, who would be angry with me if she knew. I suppose I'll give it a few weeks, then have another chat with

Bryony. If she's still on it, it will be decision time.

This is hard for Alban. He's giving his granddaughter a chance to straighten herself out but, if she doesn't, when the crunch comes, he'll have to make up his mind as to whether to go for the 'tough love' approach. If your grandchild is in this situation, only you can decide how to handle it. But whichever route he chooses, Alban has been able to keep up a dialogue with Bryony because, instead of berating her, he's discussed the issues with her, treated her as if she were a grown-up with a right to her own views. This means he'll be able to broach the subject with less risk of Bryony blocking him off.

Strengthening the Bond

At this stage of their lives, all youngsters, whether they're having specific problems or not, need extra emotional back-up. They don't sit on your knee any longer, but that doesn't mean they won't want a hug now and then. They might not show it, but you can bet your boots they'd like it – as long as you don't try to do it when they're with their friends. They'll respond to you if you don't make a big deal out of everything. Casual chats, no pressure, will be appreciated by youngsters who are suddenly finding that life is full of pressure. It helps if you've seen a lot of your grandchildren as they've been growing up. The precedent will already be established for them to spend time with you, and they'll seek you out, even if they're currently living away.

These days it's easy to keep in touch by email, which is less demanding on their time than phone calls or letters. If you send the occasional email – it doesn't have to be long – giving them a bit of news, they're quite likely to answer it. It's private, no one knows what they're saying, but *they* know you'll be totally interested in anything and everything they tell you, however trivial. No one can resist that.

The important thing is to be confident. Assume they still regard you as an interesting person. In fact, that should be easier for this generation of grandparents to do than previous ones, because we're so young physically, and in our heads. Unlike our predecessors, who sat and watched from the sidelines, we've played an active role in their lives until this point. We have a big start, so why drop back?

Sandy and Beverly have three teenage grandchildren. Sandy says, 'The grandparent–child relationship is very precious – it's special, but it time-expires. When they're older, all you can do is to remember their birthdays, and send them the odd fiver from time to time. We know they've got a life to lead, and we're not talking their language any more. So it was wonderful when our eighteen-year-old granddaughter, Iris, proved that we do matter. She and her first serious boyfriend invited us out for a meal so we could meet him. We were delighted. It's lovely to think she still regards us as significant people in her life.' Sandy's right: of course you can't muscle in on their life, but if you get the balance correct, they'll want you to stay a part of it.

Staying in the picture can be easier than you think. Before they even reach their teens, you could start talking to them about *yourself*: your job or career, your hobbies and interests. They won't know much about this unless you tell them. It will serve two purposes: it ups your cool factor, and helps them see you as a rounded person with a role in the wider world, not just in the granddad or grandma dimension they've always known. They won't underrate you – they'll be fascinated to discover what you can do, or have done.

Ghislaine and Christopher have two grandchildren, aged five and nine. Ghislaine says: 'Our daughter bought them a

CD of hits of the 1960s, and they know all the tunes and words by heart. One day when we arrived at their house, they were singing along to it and we joined in. They looked up in amazement and said, "How do *you* know this?" I told them it was *our* music – these were the exact songs we listened to when we were young. It took them a minute to get their heads round it, but then we had a mini-disco. They thought it was amazing – and very funny – that we knew how to rock and roll!' This is a perfect example of why it's good to show yourselves in a different light. As your grandchildren grow up, it will add to their understanding of you as a person, not a fossil. Joel and Katherine found this when their eldest grandchildren were around ten. Katherine remembers: 'They're all excellent swimmers and love the water, so one day we surprised them by showing them pictures of us scuba diving. They'd known on some level we were divers, but had never joined up the dots. We talked to them about it, showed them books, and developed their interest. They like snorkelling, and we hope, eventually, we'll be able to give them a taste of what it's like to dive. Then, if we're really lucky, they might actually be able to dive with us one day. That would be a thrill.'

Whatever your skill, you can impart it. Brenda is good at sewing, and her eldest granddaughter is beginning to take an interest. 'Agatha is only eight, but she's already interested in clothes – not just current fashion, but other periods, too. She started having a go with a needle and thread: she was dying to make something herself. Her mum, my daughter, is a keen sewer, and so she and I are both helping Agatha along. She loves it and, as she gets older I'll get a kick out of passing on what I've learned.' This works whether it's bird-watching, or a talent for DIY. Children are like sponges: they soak up everything, and it's great to think they'll have a life-long skill or interest they can put down to you.

There are other ways you can stay in their lives. Melvin and Lindsay are in their eighties, and Lindsay suffers badly from arthritis. Melvin says: 'Lindsay can't get about very well, and needs quite a lot of help in the house. Our granddaughter is in her early twenties, and comes to do our ironing. We pay her a little bit, so we all benefit: we get the ironing done, and spend time with her, and she gets some extra cash. It's good for everyone.'

A Link With the Past

Grandparents and great-grandparents fulfil another vital role: we're a walking, talking, history book, a living link with the past – the years we span between us have seen innumerable changes in the world. We can offer eye-witness accounts of momentous events, and we go still further back, because we know *our* grandparents' stories about events in the early part of the twentieth century. So we can bring to life two world wars, the atom bomb, the final years of the British Empire, the abdication, the Depression, Korea, Vietnam, the moon landings, flights to Mars, the Berlin Wall – we, or our parents or grandparents, were there when they happened.

We can tell our grandchildren or great-grandchildren about them from a personal perspective; the mass of detail in our memory banks will provide valuable insights, a richness that history books can't offer.

It's profoundly worthwhile to sit down with your grand-children and make a proper record – adding a commentary to what they're covering at school. Great-grandparents were perhaps children at the end of the First World War; perhaps fought in the second, or maybe worked as a land girl, or in a munitions factory. By contrast, we were around in the post-war years, during the space race and the Cold War.

Rosalie's sister, Henrietta, had seven grandchildren. Rosalie says, 'She was wonderful. She had a special, individual relationship with each of her grandchildren; they sought her advice about their homework, even, latterly, on their dissertations. They discussed everything with her. One of her grandsons took a tape recorder round to her flat so she could tell him about her life, and all the changes that had occurred during her part of the twentieth century. She had a wonderfully retentive memory. When she died he gave a copy to each member of the family. It's a fantastic slice of history. A lot of it made me cry, but it's something very precious for future generations.' Rosalie's right – this is a priceless record. It's wonderful too, for Henrietta's grandchildren to be able to hear her voice again.

Denis's great-grandson Damon was working on a school project about the formation of the Home Guard during the Second World War.

I found Damon watching *Dad's Army* one day, and I asked him why – he's twelve, and it didn't strike me as his kind of programme. He said they were doing the subject at school and his teacher had suggested it would be a good thing to look at. I said if he wanted to know about the Home Guard, he could always ask me – my dad was in it. Damon was thrilled to bits, and started asking me all kinds of questions. I told him everything I could remember, including a few funny stories my dad had told me. He loved those. And I dug out some old stuff of my father's, too – photos, the odd document. I'd had them all these years, but never thought to talk to Damon about his great-great-granddad – it seemed so remote. Anyway, we made up a scrap-book, a diary of a

Home Guard soldier, and he took it to school. He got high marks, but I reckon the best thing was the way it made us good mates. We often have a chat now, about the war. I was at the Normandy landings, and I have plenty to tell him. He isn't doing anything on it at school, he just likes to hear about it. But I bet it'll come in handy one of these days.

What Denis is doing is very important – he's passing on information that would have been lost for ever. Whatever your history, it's vital to do this; don't let the past die with you. Encourage future generations to do the same, and keep alive a real perspective on events. It's not just the big things that matter, it's all the social history even as recently as your own childhood when coal or milk or vegetables were still sometimes delivered by horse and cart; possibly you had no bathroom, just a tin bath in front of the fire and a privy in the yard. You can talk about the tail end of rationing, pounds, shillings and pence, how cheap things were (you'll wow them with that). What games did you play? What toys did you have? There's so much to tell – the kind of clothes you wore (boys in short trousers until they were *eleven*) the food you ate, and the way houses were cleaned. The sheer hard labour of housework is another one that will blow their socks off – think of your grandma, maybe even your mother, doing the washing in a tub, with a rubbing board. What did *your* grandparents do for a living? Were they coal miners? Did your mother work in a mill? Were they very poor? What was that like for them? Maybe they were gentry, drove a pony and trap and had a maid. The list is endless, and the deeper you dig, the more interesting it will be. In fact, children don't need to be teenagers to appreciate any of this – little ones love stories of the 'olden days', by which, sadly, they mean your youth . . .

You can combine all this with family photos, to show them the people you're talking about. They'll laugh at the weird hairstyles and funny clothes, and the pictures will give them even more to talk about. You'll pick out likenesses ('You've got your great-great-grandma's nose'); you'll tell stories, make them three dimensional; you can parade their family before them in a fascinating kaleidoscope. This is better by far than even the most elaborate museum set; this is real, because it's *their* story – their family who lived like this, not strangers.

And even very recent history has its own charm. Children and teenagers alike love to look at pictures of when their own parents were small, and you were in your prime – let's face it, there's plenty to amuse. The iconic 1960s might still look fresh – grandma in a mini skirt! But the 1970s and 1980s style failures are bound to make them laugh – Granddad with an Afro and clogs, Mum at six in flares and a poncho . . .

Estelle and Jethro are marking their family photographs with names, specifically for their grandchildren. Jethro says, 'Estelle has a big family – I haven't sorted them all out myself, and we've been married for forty years. Her mother was one of eight, several of whom married brothers and sisters in another big family, so the ramifications are totally beyond me. Now Estelle's mum is dead, I think it's time we got out the box of ancient pictures and wrote names on the backs. It will make things clearer for everyone. There's a large Edwardian photograph of Estelle's great-grandma on our landing wall. She's a fearsome-looking woman who was, apparently, a butcher. I know our grandchildren haven't a clue who she is, and our children probably don't know either, so we've decided to put a label on the back of the frame. After all, at some point after we're gone, the children are bound to ask about her.' This is a good idea, but it's worth talking about her now, too. Otherwise, when they do come to read that label, there will be a lot of unanswerable questions.

Albert and Latisha are doing this, too. They came to the UK from Tobago when they were married, forty-five years ago, and, although they've been back from time to time, their grandchildren have never been there. Latisha says, 'Our parents are all dead now, and our grandchildren never met them, so we've made a point of telling them about their ancestors, and what life was like for them on the island. We have plenty of photographs, and we talk about the people in them. We've drawn a family tree, so there's a record. It isn't fancy, but they do like to go through it and have us tell stories about the names on it. You'd think at sixteen and seventeen they'd be too grown-up for all that, but not a bit of it. We're so pleased. And it's always good to have a captive audience!'

A Lasting Legacy

This is part of your legacy to your grandchildren: the gift of their past. If you don't pass it on, if you haven't already started that process with your own children, then the road back into history will end with you. This would be a tragedy, not just because of what they'll never know, but for you, too.

That's because, of all the things we do in our lives, of all the relationships we have, the one with our grandchildren is perhaps the most poignant – it's tinged with parting from the very beginning. And it's this brevity which makes it so precious. One of these days it's going to come to an abrupt end. There's no getting round it. So, naturally, you want to stay with them in the only way you can: you want to live on in their memory when you're gone. And you will. After all, you've helped them to become who they are; you've helped form their tastes, their attitudes, their values. In so many ways, big and small, you're with them every day. Of course their parents have played the major role, but don't underestimate yours. The influence you've had on their personality is profound and will be lifelong.

For one thing, if they love you, then consciously or not, you've taught them to respect the older generation. Doris and Emlyn recently celebrated their fiftieth wedding anniversary. Emlyn says, 'Our grandchildren are all students now, with lots of things going on, but they put everything off so they could come to our party. The boys even bought shirts and ties so they could be smart for us – they thought it would please us. We didn't need them to dress up, of course, but we were thrilled at the reason they did.' Doris and Emlyn are proud their grandchildren are growing up into considerate, thoughtful people. And you can be proud of yours. From their earliest days you've been there, loving and teaching them. They've absorbed your wisdom and experience from the cradle.

In years to come, they'll say, with a smile, 'My grandma always told me . . .' or 'My granddad used to swear by . . .' They'll use your recipes – fill the house with the cooking scents of their childhood, revel in them and think of you. They'll remember how you taught them to plant radishes, to swim, or ride a bike, and they'll teach their children the same way. They'll sing the songs they learned from you, and pass on the family stories you've told them to *their* children and grandchildren. Your presence in their life will enrich it, just as they've enriched yours.

So make the most of this wonderful present you've been handed. Don't miss a speck of the joy and fun. Thank the

Fates for your luck. And the bonus is, you'll still be around, a living legend, for future generations of children. What could be better? You're immortal.

TALKING TO TEENAGERS

Don't
Lecture them.

Wade in with advice unless they ask.

Blab to their parents unless you feel it's vital.

Take sides.

Make light of their problems.

Do
Tell them they can tell you *anything* – then really listen to what they say.

Reassure them you'll love them no matter what.

Keep what they say in confidence.

Try to put yourself in their place – remember how it feels to be young.

Stay calm.

KEEPING THEIR PAST ALIVE

Historical Events
Talk to your grandchildren about events during your lifetime, and that of your parents and grandparents.

Ask your grandchildren if there are any events they'd like to know about, and to tell you when they're doing history at school so you can pass on what you know.

Sit down with them and document events – your role during
the war, or as a post-war child, for example. Maybe make a
written, or taped record.

Show them photographs.

Family History

Take them through your family albums and explain who's who.
Write names on the pictures.

Tell stories about your family, and their way of life.

Sing them the songs you learned as a child.

Resources

UK

GUIDE 1: BACKGROUND READING FOR NEW PARENTS

The books and authors below represent a small fraction of what's available. They cover a range of views and will give you an idea of what the current views are. This list is a cross-section *not* a recommendation: how you feel about what they say is up to you, but at least you'll be informed.

EXPERT	APPROACH
Dr Miriam Stoppard Books include: *Baby and Child A–Z Medical Handbook* *First-Time Parents* *Complete Baby and Childcare*	Medical slant because of her background. Advice on things like how to make up formula without poisoning the baby, bathe it, etc. (NB This could be useful to grandparents who've forgotten all that and don't want to break the baby.)

(contd.)

EXPERT	APPROACH

Gina Ford
*The New Contented Little Baby
    Book*
*The Complete Sleep Guide for
    Contented Babies*
	Known as 'the queen of routine' she espouses strict timetables and divides time up into five-minute intervals. Provokes strong reactions both for and against.

Penelope Leach and Jenny Mathews *Your Baby & Child: From Birth to Age Five*	A complete contrast to the above. You carry the baby around on your hip.
Dr Spock *Baby and Childcare*	Yes, he's still out there. Updated now.
Rachel Waddilove *The Baby Book*	Nanny to both Kate Moss's babies for their first month.

Lauren Feder
*Natural Baby and Childcare –
    Practical Medical and Holistic
    Advice*
	Complementing conventional medicine with alternative therapies, plus organic baby foods, green baby products, and so on.

Janet Balarkas and Peter Walker *The Book of Baby Massage*	Step-by-step guide to baby massage.
Dr Penny Stanway *Breast Is Best*	The classic standby for mothers who want to breastfeed.

GUIDE 2: SUPPORT ORGANISATIONS FOR NEW PARENTS

Here are some of the organisations which provide information and support for new parents. They can be handy for you, too, if you want to keep up with current thinking.

ORGANISATION	WHAT IT DOES
National Childbirth Trust Enquiry line: 0870 444 8707 Breastfeeding line: 0870 444 8708 www.nct.org.uk	Charity with lots of information on baby care, breastfeeding, etc. Runs classes in breast-feeding.
The Breastfeeding Network Supporter line: 0870 900 8787	Support and informa-tion for breastfeeding women.
Cry-sis Helpline: 0207 404 5011	Helpline for parents with excessively crying babies.
Bbc.co.uk/parenting	Website with informa-tion on many aspects of parenting.
NHS Direct 0845 4647 www.nhsdirect.nhs.uk	Information on various aspects of babies' health.
Bupa	Fact sheets on things like colic, crying, breast-feeding.

GUIDE 3: WILLS, REGISTRATION
AND LEGAL ENQUIRIES

ORGANISATION	WHAT IT DOES
General Register Office England and Wales: PO Box 2, Southport, Merseyside PR8 2JD 0170 456 9824 www.gro.gov.uk Scotland: New Register House, 3 West Register Street, Edinburgh EH3YT 0131 334 0380 www.gro-scotland.gov.uk Northern Ireland: Oxford House, 49/55 Chichester Street, Belfast BI1 4HL 0289 025 2000 www.groni.gov.uk	For registry of births, deaths and marriages. Will advise on things like paternity.
Her Majesty's Court Service www.hmcs.gov.uk	Will answer questions about probate. Leaflets.
Children's Legal Centre www.childrenslegalcentre.com	Guides and publications. Booklet *What's in a Name?*
Parentline 0808 800 2222	Advice line.
Community Legal Services 0845 345 4345 www.clsdirect.org.uk	Information about registering births.
Family Rights Group www.frg.org.uk	Advice to parents and grandparents on social care services.
DirectGov www.direct.gov.uk	UK government public service information on registering and naming your baby, guide to wills and probate.

ORGANISATION	WHAT IT DOES
Citizens' Advice Bureau See local phone book www.adviceguide.org.uk	Help with all legal queries.
Grandparents Association www.grandparents-association.org.uk	Charity set up to promote rights of grandparents.

GUIDE 4: POSTNATAL DEPRESSION – FACTS AND HELP

ORGANISATION	WHAT IT DOES
Association for Postnatal Depression Helpline: 0207 386 0868	Support for mothers suffering from post-natal illness.
Perinatal Illness UK Telephone helpline being developed www.pni-uk.com	As above.
Mind (National Association for Mental Health) England and Wales: Information line: 0845 766 0163 www.mind.org.uk Scotland: Information line: 0141 568 7000 www.samh.org.uk Northern Ireland: Information line: 0289 032 8474 www.niamh.co.uk	Information, booklets, support.
The Association for Post-Natal Illness info@apni.org www.apni.org	Support for mothers with PND.

(contd.)

ORGANISATION	WHAT IT DOES
Depression Alliance www.depressionalliance.org	Website for sufferers of depression. Information packs on all aspects of PND, plus leaflets and online help. Network of self-help groups.
Meet a Mum (MAMA) www.mama.co.uk PND Helpline: 0845 120 3746	Organisation specifically for mothers with pre- and post-natal depression.
National Childbirth Trust Helpline: 0870 444 8707 www.nctpregnancyandbabycare.com	Support groups for depressed mothers.
The Samaritans Helpline: 0845 790 9090 jo@samaritans.org	Confidential helpline.

GUIDE 5: KEEPING YOURSELF UP TO DATE

ORGANISATION	WHAT IT DOES
Parentline Plus Helpline: 0808 8002222 www.parentlineplus.org	Publications, workshops, website with useful information.
National Library for Health – Child Health www.library.nhs.uk/childhealth	Information on dealing with antisocial behaviour as well as health issues.
NSPCC www.nspcc.org.uk	*Your Family* magazine. Leaflets on a variety of subjects, including discipline.
The Children Act	See pages 258, 269.

GUIDE 6: IF YOU'RE WORRIED

ORGANISATION	WHAT IT DOES
NSPCC Helpline: 0808 800 5000 www.nspcc.org.uk Asian Helpline: 0800 096 7719	Leaflet to download: *If You're Worried About a Child*. Enquiries can be dealt with in the Asian language of your choice
Childline Childline, Freepost, NATN1111, London E1 6BR Helpline: 0800 1111 www.childline.org.uk	Confidential helpline for children and adults concerned about a child. But depending on circumstances, action might have to be taken.

(contd.)

ORGANISATION	WHAT IT DOES
Department of Health Publications www.doh.org.uk	Leaflet to download: *What to Do If You're Worried a Child Is Being Abused.*
Citizens' Advice Bureau www.adviceguide.org.uk Local phone book	Fact sheets.
Brook Advisory Centre Information: 0207 284 6040 Helpline: 0800 018 5023 www.brook-org.uk	Advice for young people under twenty-five about a variety of sexual health issues, including abuse.
Social Services/Health Visitors See local phone book	If you tell them something, they will have to investigate, although this won't necessarily mean speaking immediately to the child's parents, or breaking your confidentiality.
GP Local phone book	A doctor can't ignore a communication of this kind, but your anonymity won't necessarily have to be breached.
Police – Child Welfare Local phone book	Police are duty bound to investigate, but as above.
The Children Act www.opsi.gov.uk England and Wales 1989; Scotland 1995; Northern Ireland: The Children Order, 1995.	Details of the Act and children's rights, including smacking.

GUIDE 7: INFORMATION ON ALLERGIES AND CHILD HEALTH

This is in no way a personal recommendation of the books below
– simply a small fraction of what's out there.

BOOK	APPROACH
Alice Willitts and Deborah Carter *Food Allergies and Your Child: A Practical Guide for Parents*	Advice and personal experiences.
Lucille Hammond and Lynne Marie Rominger *The Child-Friendly Allergy Cookbook*	Recipes for children with allergies.
Carolyn Humphries *Your Allergy-Free Diet Plan for Babies and Children*	Recipes and nutritional advice.
Linda Gamlin and Jonathon Brosoff *The Allergy Bible: Understanding, Diagnosing and Treating Allergies and Food Intolerances*	Advice on living with allergies, symptoms, treatments, both conventional and complementary medicine.
NHS Direct 0845 4647 nhsdirect.nhs.uk	Huge health website.

GUIDE 8: REGISTERING AS A CHILDMINDER

ORGANISATION	WHAT IT DOES
National Association of Childminders Information line: 0800 169 4486 www.ncma.org.uk	Handbook covering everything, including negotiating contracts.
Direct.gov.uk www.childcarelink.gov.uk	Website directing you to local council information on all aspects of childcare.
Grandparents Association Advice line: 0127 944 4964 www.grandparents-association.org.uk	Advice on setting up and registering as a childminder.
Government Information England: OFSTED 0845 601 4771 Commission for Social Care Inspection 0845 015 0120 Childcare Approval Scheme 0845 767 8111 Wales: Care Standards Inspectorate 0144 384 8450 Scotland: Campaign for Regulation of Care 0845 603 0890 Northern Ireland: Health and Social Services Trust Local Health and Social Care Trust Local phone book	Information on child-minding standards and registering. For information pack on becoming a childminder.

GUIDE 9: INFORMATION FOR CHILDMINDERS

ORGANISATION	WHAT IT DOES
Grandparents Association Advice line: 0845 439 585 www.grandparents-association.org.uk	Advice on benefits, grants.
Daycare Trust Hotline: 0207 840 3350 training@daycaretrust.org.uk www.daycaretrust.org.uk	National childcare charity offering help, advice and a childcare training programme, plus brochure to download.
National Literacy Trust General enquiries: 0207 587 1842 www.literacytrust.org.uk	Offers pack on communicating with your grandchildren.
Family Information Service 0207 641 7929 Local phone book under local authority	Information on childminding. Two-hour briefing session for anyone wanting to set up as a childminder.
Government Information www.directgov.uk Helpline: 0845 300 3900 Childcare Providers Helpline: 0845 300 3941 Child Benefit for England, Scotland and Wales: 0845 302 1444; for Northern Ireland: 0845 603 2000	Your entitlements – tax and benefits, grants, tax credits. Links you to Scotland and Northern Ireland too.

GUIDE 10: BRINGING UP YOUR GRANDCHILDREN – THE LAW

Here are some useful organisations to help you find out about the law regarding raising your grandchildren. The information could vary regionally. If your children wish to appoint you as guardian(s) in their will, they should see their solicitor.

ORGANISATION	WHAT IT DOES
Citizens' Advice Bureau Local phone book www.adviceguide.org.uk	Free advice and helpline on the law and your rights.
Grandparents Association Advice line: 0845 439 585 www.grandparents-association.org.uk	Advice, leaflets on all aspects of kinship care, including the law; how to find a specialist lawyer.
Office of Public Sector Information Special Guardianship Regulations 2005 England: www.opsi.gov.uk Wales: www.opsi.gov.uk/legislation/wales Scotland: www.opsi.gov.uk/acts/ Northern Ireland: www.opsi.gov.uk/si/si2005/20051109 Childcare Policy Direct Local Health and Social Care Trust www.fostering.hscni.net	The letter of the law, in all its detail.
CAFCASS – Family Court Advisory and Support Service www.cafcass.gov.uk	The law on residence, special guardianship and adoption.

ORGANISATION	WHAT IT DOES
Her Majesty's Courts Service www.hmcourts-service.gov.uk	The law on adoption, fostering, special guardianship and residence orders for England and Wales.
British Association of Adoption and Fostering England: www.baaf.org.uk for phone numbers for specific areas Wales: cardiff@baaf.org.uk Scotland: scotland@baaf.org.uk Northern Ireland: northernireland@baaf.org.uk	Information for people considering adoption or fostering. Plus information on legislation, fees, allowances.
The Fostering Network England: 0207 620 6400 Wales: 0292 044 0940 Scotland: 0141 204 1400 Northern Ireland: 0289 070 5056 www.fostering.net	Provides information, training, advice.
Adoption UK Freephone: 0800 783 4081 www.adoption.org.uk	Information line, advice, support.
Law Society: Find a Solicitor 0870 606 2555 www.lawsociety.org.uk Scotland: www.lawscot.org.uk Northern Ireland: www.lawsoc-ni.org www.solicitorsonline.com	Both these organisations will put you in touch with a solicitor who is an expert on children's law.
Your Local Authority Local phone book	Check out your social services' approach to grandparents as parents.
Children's Ombudsman Local phone book	If you're not happy with a situation, this is where to complain.

GUIDE 11: OVERVIEW OF THE MAJOR CARE OPTIONS OPEN TO GRANDPARENTS

OPTION	DETAILS
Kinship Care	This is when children are raised by members of their family other than their parents.
Parental Responsibility	Gives you all the rights, powers and duties of a parent. The birth mother will have it, and the father if they're married. If they're not married, he won't necessarily have it. Grandparents don't have, and can't apply for parental responsibility.
Residence Order Means-tested	This will enable you to keep your grandchildren until they're sixteen. Parental responsibility comes automatically, but you still share it with one or more of their parents. This means that while you can make day-to-day decisions about your grandchildren's lives, you can't make major ones unilaterally. You could be entitled to some benefits (see pages 265–6).
Special Guardianship Order Means-tested	You can apply for this if your grandchild has been living with you for three out of the last five years (not necessarily consecutively). It's more secure than a residence order because it can't be dissolved without the consent of the court, and it lasts until the child is eighteen. It doesn't eradicate the legal relationship between a child and its parents in the way that adoption does, but it does give you unilateral parental responsibility. You could be entitled to some benefits (see pages 265–6). Your children can appoint you legal guardian(s) in their will, should anything happen to them.

OPTION	DETAILS
Adoption	This is not generally favoured by the courts because it changes the legal relationship between the child and its family. It might also be considered desirable to separate the child completely from its birth parents.
Fostering	Foster-parents don't have parental responsibility – this rests with the local authority, so grandparents who foster are more vulnerable, but you are entitled to financial support – you have to make sure you get it (see below.)

GUIDE 12: BENEFITS FOR GRANDPARENTS RAISING THEIR GRANDCHILDREN

You may be entitled to some kind of benefit, maybe even local authority housing, but it's all entirely at the discretion of the local authority and, in any case, you will be means tested according to a sliding scale, You may also be entitled to tax credit. If you are foster-parents, you're definitely entitled to an allowance.

ORGANISATION	WHAT IT DOES
Grandparents Association Advice line: 0845 439 585 www.grandparents-association.org.uk	Advice on benefits and welfare.
Childcare Providers Helpline: 0845 300 3941	Advice on the childcare element of working tax credit.
Child Benefit England, Scotland and Wales: 0845 302 1444 Northern Ireland: 0845 603 2000	Claim pack.

(contd.)

ORGANISATION	WHAT IT DOES
Guardian's Allowance Unit Guardian's Allowance Unit Child Benefit Office, PO Box 1, Newcastle on Tyne NE88 1AA 0845 302 1464	Claim pack, information.
Local Authority Benefit Office Local phone book	Talk to them to see what the policy is, and what's available, in your area. It varies wildly.

GUIDE 13: SUPPORT GROUPS FOR GRANDPARENTS RAISING THEIR GRANDCHILDREN

These organisations provide groups, ongoing back-up, support and advice for parents raising their grandchildren.

ORGANISATION	WHAT IT DOES
Grandparents Association Advice line: 0845 439 585 www.grandparents-association.org.uk	Advice for grandparents as parents.
Family Rights Group Advice Line: 0800 731 1696 www.frg.org.uk	Booklet: *Second Time Around: A Guide for Grandparents Raising Their Grandchildren.*

ORGANISATION	WHAT IT DOES
The Grandparents Federation Helpline: 0127 9444 964	National charity giving advice, information and support to grandparents who are caring for their grandchildren.
Beth Johnson Foundation 01782 844 036 www.bjf.org.uk	Advocacy, advice on your rights, for grandparents raising their grandchildren.
Age Concern www.ageconcern.org.uk	Advice for grandparents as parents.
Drugscope www.drugscope.org.uk	National charity providing help and information.
National Drugs Helpline 0800 776 600 www.ndh.org.uk	Help and advice.
British Association of Adoption and Fostering England: 0289 031 5494 www.baaf.org.uk Wales: cardiff@baaf.org.uk Scotland: scotland@baaf.org.uk Northern Ireland: northernireland@baaf.org.uk	Information and advice for people considering adoption or fostering, plus information on fees, allowances.
The Fostering Network www.fostering.net England: 0207 620 6400 Wales: 0292 044 0940 Scotland: 0141 204 1400 Northern Ireland: 0289 070 5056	Provides information, training, advice.

GUIDE 14: THE LAW ON ACCESS TO YOUR GRANDCHILDREN

OPTION	DETAILS
Your rights	Grandparents have *no* automatic right of access to their grandchildren. This applies equally to step-grandparents, who are regarded in law in exactly the same way as grandparents.
Who can prevent you from having access?	Parent(s) with parental responsibility (see page 264) have the right to prevent you from having access to your grandchildren. If the custodial parent remarries, and the new step-parent adopts, then the latter gains parental responsibility and the divorced parent loses it, so the adoptive parent can prevent you seeing your grandchildren. The court can issue an order forbidding you access if they believe contact with you will be bad for the child. If your grandchild is in care, then, depending on what kind of care, the local authority will have either shared parental responsibility with the child's parent(s) (e.g. if the child is fostered), or total parental responsibility. If the latter, then under certain circumstances they have the right to turn you down without going to the court.
What can you do about it?	In all the situations above, if the custodial parent isn't sympathetic, try mediation. If these fail, your only recourse is to apply to the court for contact.
What can the local authority do?	Social services can arrange mediation for you with the custodial parent(s). For a child in care, the local authority has a statutory duty to promote contact with the child's family unless it would be harmful for the child.

OPTION	DETAILS
What kinds of contact can the court award?	**Direct contact** involves meeting the child for a specified number of times a month or year, maybe including overnight stays. The court may leave the details to the individuals, or decree what contact there will be. **Indirect contact** means no meetings, but contact through emails/phone calls/presents/letters/birthday cards.

GUIDE 15: ACCESS TO YOUR GRANDCHILDREN – CONTACTS AND SUPPORT

For more information regarding adoption, see Chapter 5, and page 265. Remember that the law may vary between England, Wales, Scotland and Northern Ireland.

ORGANISATION	WHAT IT DOES
The Children Act www.opsi.gov.uk/acts	The law, in detail, for the UK.
Law Society Children Panel 0870 606 12 555 www.lawsociety.org.uk www.solicitorsonline.com	List of accredited solicitors who are expert on children's law.
Citizens' Advice Bureau Local phone book	Free advice on the law.
Community Legal Service Direct 0845 345 4345 www.clsdirect.org.uk	Finding a solicitor; advice on legal aid.
Grandparents Association Advice line: 0127 944 4964 www.grandaprents-association.org.uk	Advice and leaflets on the law and procedures; booklet on arguments to use.

(contd.)

ORGANISATION	WHAT IT DOES
Family 2000 www.family2000.org.uk	Advice and information.
National Society for Children and Family Contact www.nscfc.com	Works to foster family contact.
Grandparents Plus 0208 981 8001	Advice and leaflets on every aspect of contact, and the law.
Children's Information Service 0207 641 7929	Advice and information.
National Family Mediation England and Wales: 0117 904 2825 www.nfm.u-net.com Family Mediation Scotland: 0845 119 2020 www.familymediationscotland.com	Will give you the number of your nearest mediation centre.
Families on Divorce www.ondivorce.co.uk	Has a section for grandparents.
Parentline Plus 0808 800 2222 www.parentlineplus.org.uk	Leaflet: *Grandparents in Stepfamilies.*
Basic Skills Agency www.basicskills.co.uk/resources	Leaflets on staying in touch, postcards for your grandchildren to send to you.
Grandparents Apart (GASH) 0141 882 5658 www.grandparentsapart.co.uk	Self-help group for grandparents deprived of their grandchildren, helpline, drop-in centres, mediation, meetings.

ORGANISATION	WHAT IT DOES
Families Need Fathers 0870 760 7496 www.fnf.org.uk	Information/fact sheets for grandparents with no access to their grandchildren, mediation.
Adoption Information Line www.adoption.org.uk	The law and related information.

GUIDE 16: APPLYING TO THE COURT FOR ACCESS TO YOUR GRANDCHILDREN

This is a very broad outline of what happens. It's advisable to appoint a solicitor.

- First, you must take legal advice and find a solicitor who specialises in this field – you can apply for legal aid, but it is means tested.
- Apply for leave to apply for contact.
- Even if you're given leave, this doesn't presume you will be entitled to contact.
- The decision should be based on the child's best interests.
- Next, apply for contact – this involves you setting out the reasons why it would be a good thing, for example: you've had continuous contact with your grandchild, who will miss you; he/she has already 'lost' one parent, and shouldn't lose grandparents too; etc. Your solicitor will be of material help in preparing your argument and evidence. You may want to include the statements of witnesses.
- You attend a preliminary hearing, which will decide how the case will proceed and sets a date for a full hearing.
- At the full hearing you will be asked to speak, along with any itnesses.
- The court takes into account the wishes of your grandchild.
- There will be court fees to pay – which, again, you may be given help with, subject to a means test.
- If you're unhappy with any part of the outcome, you can apply to your Ombudsman – the number will be in the local phone book.

Australia

Support groups, charities and other organisations may be state or territory-wide, rather than national, so where appropriate the links below will take you to websites that provide you with what's available where you live, or they will point out where a number or address can be found in your local telephone directory. Local government rules, regulations and practices may vary from region to region, and from state to state or territory, so it's vital that you check out your local situation.

ORGANISATION	WHAT IT DOES
www.seniors.gov.au	Government source of information relating to grandparents. Details of support groups across Australia for grandparents raising a grandchild, resources for carers, where to go for help on all issues, including family violence. Fact sheets and help lines. Help with your rights as a grandparent, financial matters, legal issues and legal aid, plus advocacy.
Council on Ageing (COTA) www.cota.org.au 0882320422 or 1800182324, plus local offices.	A major seniors' organisation, with independent bodies in all states and territories. Offers information on issues relating to grandparents.
Early Childhood Australia Inc www.earlychildhoodaustralia.org.au	Masses of information regarding child health and development. Australian Journal of Early Childhood, plus Every Child magazine. Grandparents' views on childcare, newsletter. Information on child protection.

(contd.)

ORGANISATION	WHAT IT DOES
Grandparents Australia Inc www.grandparents.com.au	An umbrella for a collection of organisations across Australia, to promote the role and needs of grandparents and grandchildren. Information for grandparents raising grandchildren, lists of support groups nationwide.
Department of Families, Housing, Community and Indigenous Affairs www.fahcsia.gov.au	Report: *Grandparents Raising Their Grandchildren* commissioned by the Minister for Children and Youth Affairs. Information on benefits for grandparents, plus details of kinship care, adoption, fostering, child abuse.
Family Court of Australia www.familycourt.gov.au	Brochures and kits on various aspects of family law, plus information on costs.
Family Law Australia www.afccnet.org	Finding specialist legal help.
Citizen's Advice Bureaux www.cab.au Local phone book	Helpline and advice on all aspects of the law.
Registry of Births, Deaths, and Marriages Local phone book	How to register a birth, plus the law on a wide variety of topics, including wills and guardianship.
Family Relationships Online www.familyrelationships. gov.au	Advice on resolving family disputes both when families are together, and after divorce or separation. Information for grandparents.

ORGANISATION	WHAT IT DOES
Australian Breast-feeding Association www.breastfeeeding.asn.au	Information, features and advice on breastfeeding.
Parenting and Child Health www.cyh.com	Detailed advice on topics like breast-feeding, allergies, new mums, post natal depression.
Post Natal Depression www.health.ninemsn.com.au	Information on PND
PND counsellors www.bubhub.com.au	Finding a counsellor, plus helplines and support groups region by region.
Australian Society of Clinical Immunology www.allerg.org.au	Detailed information on childhood allergies.
Samaritans www.samaritans.org.au Local phone book	Helpline for anyone in need of someone to listen.
Carers Australia www.carersaustralia.com.au	Information and support for carers

Republic of Ireland

The laws in the Republic of Ireland are very close to those in the UK, but there are differences, and they may also vary regionally. As with the UK, local authority policies will almost certainly differ around the country, both in their detail and in how they're implemented, so it's best to check.

Because of the similarities in law, many of the support groups, contacts and links in the UK guides will be relevant in the Republic of Ireland, and some of them will have branches in Ireland, so it's worth checking them out, especially since the situations grandparents can find themselves in are much the same in both countries.

The organisations below are all operational in the Republic of Ireland.

ORGANISATION	WHAT IT DOES
General Register Office www.groireland.ie	Registering births
Government departments and statutes www.irishstatutebook.ie	Database from which you can download any statute, including The Children Act, Adoption Act etc
Office of the Minister for Children www.omc.gov.ie	Policies and legislation concerned with child welfare and protection. Plus information on foster care.
The Adoption Board/Adoption Authority of Ireland www.adoptionboard.ie 01 2309 300/906	Detailed information on the law regarding adoption.
Citizens' Information www.citizensinformation.ie www.comhairle.ie Locall 1890777121	Information on social services – includes everything from grandparents' rights of access to grandchildren, to fostering, adoption, guardianship, kinship care.

(contd.)

ORGANISATION	WHAT IT DOES
Samaritans Local phone number	Helpline
National Society for Children and Family Contact www.nscfc.com	UK based but applicable to Republic of Ireland. Support/advice/help/advocacy for grandparents, especially those denied access to their grandchildren, or those who want to bring them up.
Grandparents Apart www.grandparentsapart.com	Support and information regarding all types of kinship care.
Carers' Association, Ireland www.carers.ireland.com Freephone 1800240724	National volunteer organisation for carers. Local centres have information packs on many subjects relating to caring.
Grandparents Action Group www.gaguk.netroup	Promotes awareness of grandparents' lack of legal rights, and provides advice and support on many issues of grandparenting.
Seniors Network www.seniorsnetwork.co.uk/grandparents	Information on many subjects related to grandparenting.

South Africa

ORGANISATION	WHAT IT DOES
Family and Marriage Association of South Africa (famsa) www.famsa.org.za	Organisation supporting family life. Counselling, advocacy, information for families coping with divorce.
Marriage and Family Life Renewal Ministry www.marfam.org.za Tel: 011 7895 449	Catholic organisation offers information and workshops on issues like family rights and children's rights. Monthly newsletter 'Family Matters', and quarterly magazine 'Marriage and Family Living'.
Radio Veritas DSTV Channel 71	Catholic radio station has a programme called 'Family Matters' discussing family issues including the role of grandparents.
South Africa Depression and Anxiety Group www.sadag.co.za	Mental health line 011 2426 396 Information and help line dealing with all forms of depress, including Post Natal Depression.
Lifeline Southern Africa www.lifeline.org.za	Equivalent to The Samaritans – for those in need of someone to talk to in a crisis.
Childline 0800 055555	24-hour free counselling and information on children's rights.
African Charter for the Rights and Welfare of the Child www.africa-union.org/child	The charter, verbatim.

(contd.)

ORGANISATION	WHAT IT DOES
The Constitutional Court of South Africa www.concourt.gov.za	Information and publications on the law – sections on family life, discipline of children, HIV/AIDS, child support.
The Public Protector www.concourt.gov.za	An independent investigator of complaints against the government.
Age-in-Action (South Africa Council for the Aged) www.age-in-action.co.uk	Contact them for details of organisations providing help and information for grandparents.
Child Welfare South Africa www.childwelfaresa.org.za	Umberella body for organisations protecting the interests of children and families. Information on a wide variety of issues, including child abuse, benefits, your rights.
Department of Social Development www.dsd.gov.za	Information on adoption, child support, HIV/Aids, plus links to Children's act and Older Persons' Act
Department of Justice www.doj.gov.za	Helps families reach agreement on issues like custody, access and guardianship.
Citizens Advice Bureaux www.cab.org.za	Free advice and help on many issues, including the law, and family matters.

Index

bad behaviour 61–2
  and the birth of a new sibling
    36–8
  discipline 75, 77, 82–3, 102–4
  and family break-up 206
bed rest 41–2
bedtime routines 61
benefit system 145–6, 152, 265–6
birth
  registering 43
  stresses of 44
  trends 15–16
boarding school 59–60
breakages 96–7
breaks, for parents 89–92
bringing up your grandchildren
    144–66, 262–7
  and adoption 146, 147–9, 264
  and the benefit system 145–6,
    152, 265–6
  care options 264–5
  fostering 145, 264
  legal issues 262–3
  parental responsibility 264
  residence orders 144–5, 152, 154,
    156, 157, 264
  special guardianship orders 145,
    152, 264
  support groups for 266–7
bullying 236

C
Canada 198–9
cancer 94
cannabis 237–8
care plans 151–2
child abuse 69, 153–4, 236
child health issues 259

child-proofing your home 134
childcare, providing 121–62, 4
  addressing your own needs
    127–33, 157–60
  becoming parents to your
    grandchildren 144–60, 262–7
  challenges of 122–3
  considerations 161–2
  costs of 136
  emergencies 138–43
  formal 136–7, 260, 155
  full-time 133–6
  refusing your children 125–6
  remuneration 136–7
  and the undervaluing of
    grandparents 149–58
childhood, reliving through your
    grandchildren 87–8
childminders 121
  information for 261
  registering as 136–7, 155, 260
Children Act 1989 74, 144, 214
children's wishes 214
Christmas 112–18, 120, 208
close relationships
  drifting apart of 187–8, 190–1
  maintaining 163–92
clustering 180
confidence 187–8
consistency 82–4, 86, 101–2,
    102–3
see also continuity of care
contact
  not wanting 93–4
  without parents 88–120
  see also childcare, providing
contact orders 214–15
contact registers 148